The Prayer that Sanctifies

Walking in Anointing and Power

Dr. Humphrey Uche

Forwarded by Bishop Ayo-Maria Atoyebi

Imprimatur: **Bishop Ayo-Maria Atoyebi, O.P.**
Bishop of Ilorin Diocese
September 10, 2005

The Prayer that Sanctifies
Published July, 2020

Copyright © 2020 Dr. Humphrey Uche

ISBN: 9798666542989
Imprint: Independently published

TABLE OF CONTENTS

DEDICATION

I dedicate this work to all those who are genuinely seeking God. May the revelation in this work inspire you to encounter Him, the author of all goodness.

PREFACE

Prayer is one thing everybody does in one way or the other but only a few can comfortably say I pray very well. This is evident in such questions that people ask like: …… but I cannot pray? Why is it that my prayer is not answered? How can I pray very well?; What kind of prayer do I say?; and the likes. That is also evident in the presence of many prayer houses here and there without the corresponding result coming from them.

I know that many souls are yearning for God. I know that many souls want to touch and experience God. They hunger and thirst for him just like David:

'As a deer yearns for running streams, so I yearn for you, my God. I yearn for the almighty God, for the living God; when shall I go to see your face oh God? Day and night, tears have become my food, as all day long I am mocked, "where is your God? (Ps. 42: 1-3)

Many want to commune with God like Abraham and Mother Patriarchs who had a very deep relationship and close with Him. See how Abraham interacts with the Lord, just like a close friend:

And the men turned from there and went to Sodom, but Abraham stood still before the Lord God .... Then he answered and said, 'Indeed now, I who am but dust and ashes have taken it upon to speak to the Lord. (Gen. 18:22- 27 NKJ)

Many want to experience the Glory of God – The Shekinah Glory of God; the life transforming and edifying Glory of God. Moses cried:

"I pray thee, show me the glory." (Exo. 33: 18RSV)

Truly many souls want to walk side by side with God but needed the kind of ministration Apostle Philip gave to Ethiopian Eunuch that opened his eyes (Acts 8: 26- 39). The Ethiopian Eunuch who had spent time worshipping God in Jerusalem did not understand what he was doing until Apostle Philip ministered him. The Ethiopian Eunuch said, How can I, unless someone guides me? People have continued to make the same request the Apostles made to Jesus in Luke chapter 11 verse 1 "Lord, teach us to pray". A lot has been said or the importance and the needs of prayer with very little emphasis on how to pray. This book comes to guide you in the light of the Holy Spirit, to teach and instruct to pray. It is practical. It will help you to get started until you are plunged completely into Him, who alone is the Joy of your soul. It will lead you to pray with power. It will lead you to experience the life changing Glory of God. It will help you to touch and embrace God, success at your life will never remain the same again. It will change your life forever – a complete transformation and inward renewal. Read on! I will meet you on high.

The Author

FORWARD

Amidst countless definitions of Prayer, one underlying principle runs through; namely, a medium of communication between two beings, in this case, God told us. The awesome potency of prayer cannot be over emphasized as a pertinent reference for our integral worth and development as Christians. Even Jesus, the son of God and the Second person of the Trinity never relegated to a lesser importance the pedestal of prayer in mission of salvation. Little wonder the Disciples headed, "Lord, teach us to pray". This explains to us prayer leads us beyond just the temporal and we remain caught up in the love of the one we love so much. The normal reaction of anyone is to feel is to feel a longing the   of the presence of the one we love.

Psalmist express the profundity of this earnest desire when he was; 'my soul is thirsting for God, the God of my ...... when can I enter and see the face of God' (Ps 42:2). This deep craving in man is truly and only truly satisfied by God himself. This is affirmed by St. Augustine who said that we are made for you O Lord God and our hearts shall not rest until they rest in you (The confessions).

This treatise on the prayer that sanctifies brings us from the realm of so much confusion of the complexities of prayer to its immediate translation into realities of life as they surround us. This brings so much hope as regards our youths especially in the lives of our morally degenerating Christianity, as this is coming from one of them. So, all hope is not lost yet. We have lost the place of prayers in our existence. The waves of secularism and technological advancements have swept away the venerable tenets of our lives as Christians.

In this book, Bro. Humphrey explicates the act of prayer is not only appropriated in our life within the temporal definition of time. No! It remains an ongoing process that expresses that life itself is prayer. The treatise is broken down in six chapters. The methodology here defines this as a personal experience of soul that seeks God beleaguered by the constant turmoil of life. This is a recurrent aspect in every Christian life. Like someone our said, 'if you do not experience tough times in your Christian life and all you have roller coaster ride though, then have better checked up your life.' That life is fraught with woes and dialectics of solution proposals, confusing decision to be made here and there is no news. Man gets so taken up by the undercurrent of problems and lost in this sea of confusion. The devil beclouds our vision. These opposing situations must be converted into challenges rather than a ground to become tepid in some cases lose our faith.

Bro Humphrey exhorts us on some aspects of prayer which we must make our own. We must learn not just to pray aright. This enunciates that we sometimes pray amiss. There is need for a cooperation between God and us. This is because he has plans for us all. We must seek to unravel this by the help of his Spirit. Time and time again, our plans do not seem to conform to what God has in stuck for us. We can never come to understanding the heart of God except we approach him through prayer. Prayer is not all about us, but about God too. We however not come to conclusion that the only basis that ratifies God's answer to our prayers is either how well we have prayed or how worthy we are in His sight. We are encouraged to persevere. This is paramount if we must arrive. The gift of an ardent faith and ultimate trust in the providence of God for us is what we must ask or since without this we cannot please God.

There is absolutely no doubt in my that this write-up has obvious relevance to life as Christians in our world today. You may not find in total agreeable but this has been a worthwhile gesture by such a young man to bring God so close to us and make us develop an interpersonal relationship with him in a very profound, reflective and thoughtful sense. If this write-up revives just a single soul for God, then it is worth even more than the effort put into it.

Start something today! Never say it's too hard or God does not seem to answer. The Grace of God can only build on nature.

I recommend you to the intercession of Mama Maria our Blessed Mother, the Mother of God. Wishing you fruitful reading.

+ Ayo-Maria O.P.
Bishop of Ilorin

CHAPTER ONE

INTRODUCTION

Prayer is the way of Jesus. It is the way of the Saints. It is the weapon of the elect. Situations bow when we pray. The impossible become possible. A man of prayer never fails. It is the power of Christians unto salvation. If you examine the biography of those whose lives made great impact for God, (other Theresa, Mahatma Gandhi, Pope John Paul 11) you will see in each case that they were people of prayer.

The force on earth or beyond, either that of the military of the scientific circle can equal the power of prayer, for prayer controls the world. Prayers bring things into existence and makes mountains quake and leave the foundations. In fact, is the key to every good thing God holds in stock for us. It unlocks all blessings. The Bible sums it up.

Do not worry about anything; but tell the almighty God all your needs in Prayer and petition shot through with thanksgiving (Philippians 4:6)

Everyone who asks will receive; everyone who seeks finds; everyone who knocks the door will open for him. (Mat 7:8)

But how do we unlock these blessings in Prayer?

Prayer, I know, is not a new term. You may have been praying in one way or the other for man can't stop praying, but of what need is the mere saying of prayer if it doesn't achieve it desired end? What I preach here is a deeper relationship with God, a prayer of union. It is because the Apostles needed something deeper than what they were doing that made them to request that Lord teaches them to pray (Lk 11:1). So, when I said "Pray" I don't mean your routine prayer. I do not mean your traditional worship. I do not mean your church ceremony or your weekly fellowship. No, (they are good) but I mean something deeper, a personal relationship with God, dwelling in him, becoming or with him. And until we do this, we will never radiate his glory. Remember that is what you are created to be, an image of God.

But wait a minute; who is God to you? .... that great King that lives far away in heaven. Oh, common you need to change that idea! Abraham would say – "he is my friend.

What is Prayer?

I want to prayerfully start this topic. In writing this, I do not intend to do that work of a Sunday school teacher or catechism instructor. No; if I want to do that I couldn't be writing because I know you have a lot of problem out there and you can even say your prayers by heart. All I want to do here is to lead you to encounter Holy Spirit who will both teach you to pray and be in you praying.

We do not know how to pray as we should, but the Holy Spirit himself intercedes for us with inexpressible groans. (Roman 8:26)

So prayerfully study this; find yourself a quiet corner; rid yourself of the worldly noise and allow the Spirit to speak to you as I lead you to encounter him.

Let me start by presenting this story of a little college student, Angela, to you. This will help clear some negative understanding to prayer, which is a problem to spiritual growth and set you on the right pedestal for what is to come. Angela was finding it difficult to passing her school examination. One day, she met the Pastor and requested for prayers. The man of God in utmost concern for the young lady gave her a long list of fasting and prayers to do and when to do them. In addition to that, she is to attend a regular week fellowship. The girl started off saying the prayers with the fasting attached to it exactly as her Pastor spelt out. She never missed her prayer time. No matter what she was doing, that thing must wait. Even when she was wake and sleepy, with heavy eyes, she still dragged the boll to say those prayers. She was carrying this prayer out. She said the prayers, not because she liked saying them but because, to her, it was an obligation that meant to be carried out in order to pass her examination. She cared little for her relationship with the person she was praying to (God). Her only interest was the examination and that was all.

Is there anything wrong with this kind of prayer? Let find out. Most times, what we call prayer is not prayer but simply an unfruitful laborious task. Thank God, who doesn't wait for our prayer before blessing us. As I lead through my ministry telling people that there is always an answer for every prayer, many find it difficult to understand it. Why! Because if this is true why has God not granted their request. But the question here is: what did God say? Nothing? No, God said something and is saying something, but because often our interest is on the problem and not on God. We don't often listen to him. When we place our interest wholly and solely on our problems it blinds us from seeing the solution, which is God. The Scripture says God holds our future and our fortune in his hands (Dan. 5: 24). So, the totality of man's destiny depends on God. When we allow Him to take control, our life will begin to follow His already established plan even before our creation. God says that he, alone, knows the plan he has in mind for you, plans for peace, not for disaster, to give you a future and a hope. (Jer. 29:11). That is why, the author is saying that prayer is a relationship. It is coordination. We may be busy fetching water from the ocean that we will fail to behold the ocean itself. Prayer is becoming one with Him. Then, and only then shall we be able to command and control situations. God placed man in control of creation. (Gen. 1: 28) and we cannot control the creature unless we are one with the creator. Come with me.

Understanding a concept goes a long way in putting one the disposition of mind over the concept. The Saints are saints not because they are extraordinary people, but because they understood the mystery of the kingdom and pursued it with all their heart. Martyrs accepted death for Christ sake because of the knowledge of the immense glorious destiny that awaits the elect. Fr. Tony de Mellow told this short story:

I used to be deaf. I would see people stand up and through strange gyration. They called it dancing. To it looked absurd-until one day I heard the music!

I fail to understand why saints-and lovers- behave the way they do. So, I'm waiting for my heart to come alive

You heart needs to come alive so that you will behave the music and see that which makes the saints spend hours in his presence. He is the joy of life. He the reason for our living. In our journey to unravel this immense treasure in prayer, we shall make use of this definition from the New Catholic Encyclopedia. It reads thus:

"Prayer is an act of cult by which man enter into communion with a higher, superhuman, supersensible being, somehow conceived as personal and experiences as real and present upon whose power he feels himself dependent."

Some words of the above definition are very prominent: ***"Prayer is act of cult by which man enters into communion".*** Prayer is a communion with God and the word "communion" means close relationship, friendly interaction, a dialogue and so on. Therefore, in prayer we encounter God for interaction, for a dialogue, for a discussion. Mother Theresa of Calcutta puts it like this:

Prayer is a two process, a dialogue, a discussion, you talk, he listens; he talks, you listen.

So, in prayer we enter into communion with an eternal being. We should be aware and conscious that in prayer he listens and he responds; he talks. It is no prayer when we rattle meaningless words or simply recite a memorized position of prayer absent-mindedly. When you meet a lovely friend for a friendly talk, you don't just pour out all you have in mind without listening to hear him with love and trust. St Theresa of child Jesus comments on this:

…Prayer in my own view is a close sharing between friends; it means making time frequently to be alone with him whom we know loves us.

Think of that your loving best friend, how relaxed you feel in his presence, because you confide in him, you trust him, you enjoy his presence, his presence soothes your sorrow. When your heart is troubled, one or two words from him calm you down because you know he cares. You feel happy meeting him all the time; you never joke with his instruction or advice; to you they a gold mine.

Brethren, this is just what God does for you and more than that because He understands you more than any person does – both your weakness and strength. In happiness and in sadness, he is there. He understands he whispers love and care. So, don't have any approaching him. He always welcomes you with smile. Confide in him. Relax in him. Listen to him. And turn to him for he cares. He is more than just a friend.

I know you may want to ask me why bring God to such a level of just a close friend. But I tell you the truth, that's what he is. There is a problem with the thought that God is so unapproachable like human kings and rulers whom we need a lot of protocols to see and enough energy to convince. These kinds of thoughts make us go about choosing the most rhetorical words to address God, putting ourselves in a most difficult position and situations to please him. We try to adopt a hard style to call his attention; select the best kind of prayer book we know to make him hear us; search for the kind of spiritual exercise that we were told that is working; look for the best kind of minister that can talk to him on our behalf. God isn't as hard or difficult to approach. The problem has always lied on our relationship and understanding. Whenever this relationship is smeared, every other tool becomes unproductive. When our understanding is crooked, our approach becomes faulty. When faith does not stand, nothing works – not even that has worked throughout the ages. Our Lord told this parable to teach us this:

Two men went to the Sanctuary to pray, one a Pharisee, the other a tax collector. The Pharisee stood up there and prayed this prayer to himself, "I thank you, Lord God, that I am not covetous, unjust, adulterous like everyone else, and especially because I am not like this tax collector here. I fast two times in a week; I pay tithes on all I have". The tax collector stood some meters away, not daring even to raise his face to heaven; but he beat his chest and said, "Lord God, be merciful to me, a sinner". This very man, I tell you the truth, went home again justified while the other did not. (Luke 18:10-14)

What matters most is how honest and true you are in this relationship and not the method used. Once the relationship is true every other method begins to work

Develop a close relationship with God. Approach him in simple manner. He is such a close friend that you don't need all those protocols to see. He enjoys seeing you, listening to you. I tell you, he smiles whenever he sees you and he enjoys seeing you happy. Listen to him:

When you call on me and come and pray to me, says the Lord, I shall listen to you. When you search for me, you will find me; when you search wholeheartedly for me, I shall let you find me Yahweh declares. I shall restore your fortunes ..... (Jer 29: 12- 14)

Just make a move, even as I'm speaking to you now, he is there waiting for you, what he only demands of you is only sincerity and honesty in your approach. Be yourself.

Again, I want to bring out other keywords in the above definition of prayer from the Catholic Encyclopedia. These words are supersensible, real, and present. The beginning of an effective prayer life lies in one's understanding that in prayer we talk to someone living, who is not just satisfied with hearing a voice that produces a sound, but who at all times questions the seriousness, and sincerity of the heart that prays. Prayers are addressed to God who is present and real; who knows every intention and thought of the heart that prays. In prayer, we talk to a living being; this is not an imagination or an illusion, it is true. In prayer, we talk to God who is very close to us, even closer to us than the clothes we are putting on. We are not inviting God, for instance, from heaven so that it will take him a very long time to come down or that our prayers will have travel many miles before getting to heaven, the abode of God. The truth is that God is ever-present. Since it is in him that we live, and move and take our being. (Acts 17:28). His name called Emmanuel which is God is with us. (Is 9:14).

So, in order to pray, all you have to do is to have enough faith to turn your attention to God and accept that you are in the presence of the one who is always totally present to you. This is what makes prayer difficult. When you are talking to a fellow man, something keeps your mind focused on him, at least you can see the person or hear his voice. Even when you are watching television or listening to radio or reading books, something keeps your mind focused on these objects, because at least you can see them or hear some sounds. It is different when you are doing an act of faith like prayer, you are communicating with a spiritual being – God, who is invisible but ever present. He is always there! We are not inviting him. He is there for us at every moment. The point is that, we come into his presence. We need enough faith to understand this. God is ever present but unlike physical man, we can only touch him by faith, see him with eye of faith and embrace him with the mind of faith. Let me show even a greater thing

CHAPTER TWO

UNDERSTANDING PRAYER

As I said before, it is very rampant these days to hear such statements as "I prayed but my prayer was not answered". As one walks across our streets one will observe a lot of churches with people offering different kinds of prayers and devotion but most times come out unsatisfied because their intentions were not met. People pass through terrifying experiences like "rigorous fasting", ritual bath in rivers", "burning of candles of different sorts and incenses in rivers banks'" and other terrifying rituals just in search of solutions to their problems. A lot of the so called men of God have deceived many; taken advantage of the people's miserable condition to enrich themselves; used them for their own selfish ambition, while promising them heaven and earth only for them to go back worse than before. This has led many to the point of abandoning their faith and others to suicidal thoughts because answers to such prayers and rituals were not received. They complain that they have prayed and done everything they can, but the Lord did not answer. But my question is: Is this true? The Bible says:

Up till now, you have not asked for anything in my name, says the Lord, Ask and you will receive, so that your joy may be complete. (John 16:24)

Do you hear that? Despite all the complaints of prayers unanswered, the Lord is still saying that you have not prayed; that you have not asked anything in his name. The Lord is still waiting to hear your prayers. And we know that His word is true, for Heaven and earth will pass away, but my words will never pass away say the Lord. (Mat. 24:35) and the Scripture says "I am watching to see that my word is fulfilled." The Lord's concern and interest is in answering your prayer so that your joy will be complete, but you have not prayed. But is it that you have not prayed or that you have not prayed well? St. James talks about it.

You do not receive because you do not pray and when you do pray and do not receive, it is because you prayed amiss, wanting to indulge your passions (James 4: 2b -3)

The problem is on us and not on God, who is able and ever willing to answer our prayers. The Bible says that our loving God is very able to make all graces abound to you, so that at all times in all things, having all that you need, you will abound in every good work. (2Cor. 9:8). And another Portion of the Scripture says that the Lord is able to do immeasurably more than all we ask or imagine, according to his power that is at work within us (Eph. 3:20). God is able and ever willing to answer our prayers. The only problem with our prayer according to the epistle of St. James is that we pray wrongly: **when you do pray and do not receive, it is because you prayed wrongly**. What does this mean?

Today I want to talk to you about the prayer that sanctifies; the true prayers without which one cannot please God or obtain anything from him and by which and only which we will be able to enter into the heavenly realm. There is only one thing called Prayer, every other one is counterfeit. The words of St. Francis De Sales is very prominent on this: one is given to fasting, and whilst he fasts he holds himself to be devout, although his heart is full of bitterness; and whilst he will not touch his lips with wine, nor even with water for abstinence' sake, he scruples not to sully them with his neighbour's blood in slander and calumny. Another would fain be devout because he daily repeats many prayers, although, at the same time, he gives way to angry, proud, and injurious language amongst his servants or associate. Another willingly opens his purse to give alms to the poor, but he cannot open his heart to forgive his enemies. Another forgives his enemies, but only force obliges him to do justice to his creditors. Such men may pass for devout; they are not really so. Once our devotion is not borne out of true Love, it cannot please God. Remember prayer is a relationship and where there is no love, there cannot be a true relationship.

The attention of a Priest was drawn to three of his church members who regularly visits the church, spending unusual long hours in prayers daily. On a particular occasion, he was moved by the Holy Spirit in the mood of Eli of Old (to Hannah) to speak to them. He didn't doubt the Spirit; he called three of them and began with the first person thus:

What is it that you ask of the Lord with all this seriousness? The answer came directly!

" I want my wife to die so that I can marry a better woman" Surprise! The Minister couldn't believe what he heard. How a sane person can make such a request of the Lord, but without hesitation and absolutely hiding his feeling, he told the man.

"You can now go; it has pleased the Lord to grant your request". He left with joy. On reaching home, he found his wife dead. When friends and relatives gathered for the funeral and began to recall the virtues of the woman, he realized that he had made a mistake and that it may not be possible for him to get a better woman. He ran back to the Church, begging the Lord to bring her back to life. Mistake indeed!

The Priest called the second person, an industrialist, and questioned: "what is it that you demand of the Lord?"

He didn't mince words. He told him point blank. "I want to be a millionaire". Very well then, the Priest continued, the Lord will grant your desire but must first go pay up all the arrears of salary you owe your workers. This statement made the man annoyed and he said "this is not what I bargained for; paying all those salaries will make me even poorer and he left."

The Priest turned to the third person a beautiful lady in her thirties and inquired, and the lady told him "I am begging the for a life partner, a husband. "And it has pleased the Lord to give you one," the Priest told her straight away. He now gave her the name and address of a young man whom God has revealed to him. The lady inquired about this and found out that he is not only a school dropout, but has no serious job doing at the moment. He lives on menial jobs. She couldn't comprehend it. How can the Lord give her such a man as husband? A graduate she is, with well-paid job, lowering herself to such a level. No, God can't just do that, no, it is not possible. She started another round of prayer: "God must understand, that thing is not for me.

A crooked mind can never please God; a mind who knows only himself and no other person, once he is satisfied others can go to blazes. A crooked mind can never obtain anything from him; a mind that knows only "I" and never "we"; a mind that can push, stamp, or even kill his neighbour in order to achieve his inordinate ambition. Once loves fails, nothing else stands. No wonder the words of our Lord Jesus stand very profound on this:

If you are carrying your offering to the altar of God and there remember that your neighbour has something against you, keep your offering there before the sanctuary, go and be reconciled with your neighbour first, and then come back and present your offering to God. (Mat. 5:23-24)

And again in mark 11:25 we read:

And when you pray, forgive whatever you have against your neighbour

In prayer, we seek and relate with a loving God. Since God is love, whoever that will seek him must seek him in love. And love is a sacrifice. When this special attribute of God is not in you and you seek to find him, you will seek in vain. This I command you: love one another. (John 15: 17). Therefore, one must be ready to accept this in order to establish a true relationship with God.

Most times what people go to church to seek is only what Jesus gives and never Jesus. Jesus told the Jews: You are searching for me, I am telling you the very truth, not because you understand the miraculous signs but because you ate the loaves of bread and had your fill. Do not work for food that spoils, but for food that will endure to life eternal, which the Son of Man will give you. It is on him that God the Father almighty has placed his seal of approval. The miraculous sign points to Lord Jesus Christ but still, they refused to believe in him. Lord Jesus said: the miracles I perform in the name of my Father speak for me, but you do not believe because you are not part of my sheep (Jn. 10: 25). So Brother, go beyond just the satisfaction of the material needs to embrace him who is the fullness of life himself and from whom all good things come, so that you will not beg for crumbs like the Canaanite woman (cc. Mat.15 : 27) but have a share in the Divine inheritance. The utmost goal of Christianity is the possession of Christ as our inheritance. Brother the best for you in life is to possess Christ for in him lies the fullness of grace by which we receive one blessing after another (cc. John 1: 16). If you work for food and drink, it will one day finish and you will become hungry again, but Jesus declared: I am the bread of life that comes from heaven. Anyone who comes to me will never be hungry, and he who trusts in me will never be thirsty. If you go for healing today and tomorrow you may need another one after. Fr. Stephen Njoku puts it thus: healing only comes when I am not healthy. Why can't I prevent loss of health, then I will not have the need to run around for healing, but probably for other reasons. It means then, that I have to go for God's best – health, and not his second best – healing. Fr. Njoku further buttressed this point by citing Don Double: the more we allow God's word to dwell in us, the more health we will have and that is always better than healing. If you pray for a good job today, tomorrow you may pray for a good wife or husband. When you get this, only then will your eyes open to see greater need to pray for, but he that is in Christ Jesus lacks nothing for a spring of living water shall continue to well up in him unto eternal life (cc. John 4:14). Allow Christ to lead the way and you will never lack the light of life. The Bible says: Seek first the kingdom of God and his righteousness, and all these other things will be given to you also (Matt.6:33).

We refuse to abide by the word of God and still hope and pray for the blessings that come from obeying the Word of God, it is like one trying to reap where he did not sow. You may be engaged in a fruitless labour because these things are not magic. One thing leads to another. Pattern your life according to the Word of God first, then every other thing follows. Any Pastor that is promising you blessing and healing or teaching you prosperity principles outside the word of God is either deceiving you, trying to take advantage of your desperate condition to enrich himself or leading you totally away from God. Watch your steps before you land into a pit. We are in the age where many churches have shifted emphasis from "holy living" to an earthly mastery of prosperity principle. This is because that is what people want but instead of the Church standing out as sign to guide the people, the church turned to follow them. Terrible! If you must claim God's promises, you must also live by God's principle otherwise it will be incompatible. God says: What right do you have to recite my status or take my law on your lips? You hate my teaching and reject my words. Ps. 50:16. Listen to this:

"Do not trust in misleading words and say: This is the house of the LORD, the house of the LORD, the house of the LORD! ….. But look, you are trusting in misleading words that are worthless. "will you kill and rob, indulge in adultery and perjury, burn incense to Baal and worship other gods you do not know, and then come and stand before me in this Temple, which bears my Name, and say, "We are safe'… safe to do all these evil things? (Jer. 7:3-10).

A priest seeing an old lady devoutly put one candle on the tip of the spear of Saint Michael the Archangel and another on the devil's tail, asked her: Cecilia, will you tell me what this means?" Listen, father, I have lighted a candle to Saint Michael because he is now up high and is winning, but I also light a small candle to the devil in case some day they switch roles. I am playing it safe." (J. Maurus, 1987). You are not different from Cecilia when you live in sin and still pray for God's blessing. You are not different from Cecilia when you suck your neighbour's blood and still pray for a breakthrough. It doesn't work like that. It is not magic. Therefore, your fat donation in the Church, your prayer and fasting, your membership of Church communities, or choir, your friendship with the pastor or priest cannot help you to develop an intimate relationship with God without abiding in His word. It will only make you a hypocrite and the Bible says such cannot receive anything from the Lord. So instead of blessing –God says "I will settle them with one blow after another" GNB (Is. 29:11).

Remember we said prayer is a union with God. It is a relationship with God. You cannot relate well with the person you don't know. Even when you do know the person you cannot relate well with him if you do not like him or like his ways. Dishonesty kills relationship. God's ways are forever established. When you reject his ways, plan for your life and try to bend him to your own way, there is always a problem.

God is interested in you. He is interested in establishing a lasting and true relationship with you. He has a better plan for you. (cc Jer. 29:11). Your future and fortune lies in his hands. (cc. Dan. 5:23). All he wants is that you dwell in him, in the riches of his grace so that everything will abound for you. This is not to picking crumbs and going away, but dwelling in his abundance. All you need to do is to allow him take control; total resignation to his will; to abide by his word and directions. Every other thing, he takes charge.

A Christian Brother praying to God for success in a job interview was offended when he couldn't get the job. He inquired and found out that the position was given to a man who, according to him, was living a wayward life. He couldn't understand this. A month later he started a personal foodstuff business which wasn't moving as he expected, but little did he know that the Lord was preparing him for something great. Close to one year in the business he got a contract to supply rice to two major hotels in the locality. This began his success story. Today his an employer and never an employee and he learnt his greatest lesson when he found out that the company into which he sought to be employed folded one year later and all the staff were laid off. Often, people approach God with different intentions. Pressing him to do it their own way, whether it is right or wrong. When you want it your own way, whether it is right or wrong. When you want it your own way it blinds you to the Lord's direction, instruction and guide. The Lord may be leading a man in a better path or preparing him for a better future or he may have allowed a situation for a purpose, to teach a lesson but because he is often blind to the Lord's work, he sticks stubbornly to his own ideas which often land him into troubles and regrets.

So, true union or relationship with God is to become one with him. That his thought will be your thought, his ways will be your ways, you will live because he lives and nothing but for him. Your words will be his words because you speak not of your own, but that which you hear from him. His glories will be seen in you because you live not for yourself but for him alone. You will cry and He will answer because His Spirit dwells in you, and this is what I consider as the prayer that sanctifies; the true prayer and unless we reach this stage will never radiate his glory which he originally purposed for our lives. The Scriptures puts it even clearer:

If you abide in me and my words dwell in you, then you may ask for whatever you need and it will be given to you. It is to the glory of God my Father that you should be my disciples and bear much fruit. I have loved you just as the Father in heaven has loved me. Abide in my love. If you obey my commandments you will abide in my love, just as I abide in his love. (John 15:7-10)

The ardent prayer of a virtuous person is very powerful. (James 5: 16b)

Trust in the Lord, our God, and do good that you may live in the land and be secured. Delight in the Lord God and he will give you your heart's desire. Commit your life to the Lord God and trust that he will act and make your integrity shine like the dawn, your salvation like the noonday. Be still before the Lord and you will possess the land. (Ps.37:3-9)

The Original God's purpose for our life is for us to increase and multiply (Gen. 1:28). So, whatever stands against your attainment of this divine ordination for you is not of God. Therefore, stand and fight it. Adam and Eve lost the paradise when they neglected and rejected the counsel of the Lord and followed that of the devil. (Gen.3). The prodigal son missed the way when he neglected and followed his own way. (Lk 15). So, the moment we begin to live in Jesus and for Jesus, we will begin to control and command situations just as he did.

They were astonished and said to each other: what kind of man is this, that even the storms and the sea obey him? (Mat. 8:27.)

Rev. Fr. Stephen Njoku, in his book, walking in the Power and the Glory summaries this thus:

The truth is this: everything goes tumbling down because people weave a network of evil against themselves. And when their cups are full, and they drink bitterness, they run about looking for a way out.

Yet their misery is their handiwork. Give them the chance to talk, all they give is the devil's report of woes upon woes, tales of the evil in their life.

And this is exactly what is happing today. People don't want to repent of their evil deed, they reject God's ways, bluntly follow their own ways, yet they want God's blessing, the blessings of obedience to God's words. The result is that they run into evil preachers who take advantage of them for their own selfish purpose. Fr. Njoku continues:

In an attempt to solve their problems, troubled people run to and fro and run into the hands of dupes, heartless charlatans and invaders. I beg your pardon, I would think that, in circumstances like this, these people need someone who can tell them the truth, whether they want to hear it or not.

In another portion of the same book Fr. Njoku offers a solution.

… pray to be lifted to the mountain peak of the victory of Jesus; that you may be given the divine ability to have a share in the inheritance of the sanctified. Adjust your life to the truth revealed by God in his word. When you

know the truth and live by it, you will enjoy a life of freedom. You may not need deliverance prayer after all. Begin now to adjust your life to the word of God, and you will see the difference.

This is very important. You ought to adjust your life to the truth of the Gospel, for that will put you in the right frame for your blessings. It may be a waste of time spending long hours in the church praying, only to suck the blood of your neighbours after, cheat him, or treat him like an animal. Why fast yourself to death, when you oppress those under your care, refuse to pay your debt, and move with a chip on your shoulder ready to bite any person that comes your way? It may not do you any good to jump from the bed of fornication to the crusade ground, only to start claiming God's promises, singing his blessings. No, it doesn't happen that way, it is not magic. Wash yourself first. Those promises and blessings are for the children of the inheritance. Are you? Instead of spending so much time looking for the reigning prayer book or for that popular preacher that is moving the land, spend time adjusting your life to the Gospel of Christ. Once you are one with him, every other thing follows. Set your heart on his kingdom first, and God's saving justice, and all these other things will be given you as well. (Mat.6:33). Your fat donation in the church may not do you any good, if you refuse the Lord to correct you. The Lord already has a set plan for your life, all you need to do is to stick to his direction and instructions and you will walk into it. You will reap the blessings. The Bible is very emphatic on this:

Why have we fasted, if you do not see, why mortify ourselves if you never notice? Look, you pursue your own pleasure on your fasting days, and you cheat all your workers; …. Fasting like yours today will never make your voice heard on high ….. Is that what you call fasting, a day acceptable to Yahweh? Is not this the sort of fast that pleases me: to break unjust fetters, to undo the thongs of the yoke: to let the oppressed go free, and to break all yokes? Is it not feeding the hungry, and sheltering the homeless; and when you see someone lacking clothes, to clothe him, and not turn away from your own family? Then your very light will shine out like morning and your pain be quickly healed. Saving justice will go before you and the Lord's glory will come behind you. Then you will cry for help and Yahweh will answer; you will call and he will say, 'I am here. *(Is.58:3-9)*

You are serving a God of love. Live in love and you will be his friend.

When we approach God the way we approach Juju priests, Pagan Idols or Magicians it becomes a problem. Pagan idols are wicked gods. The same could be said of its priests. This is because they are formed by man, out of his wicked and evil inclination. Since it is a direct activity of man, it is bent to execute man's inordinate ambitions without question. Even when there is such a question, mere rituals can avert it. A man who wants to eliminate his neighbours for money-making rituals must find an idol or juju priest who will dance to his tune. A man who wants his way even to the detriment of his own life or that of his neighbour cannot be stopped as long as he is ready to pay the price.

This is not so with our God who is all loving and has no evil in him. Like a good father, he questions not only the seriousness of the mind that prays but also the integrity of his action. So, pattern your life according to His. Wipe your mind of all evil inclinations. Live by His revealed word and you will begin to enjoy life for that is His purpose for your life.

When you live in righteousness, your prayer becomes efficacious for "the prayer of a righteous man is powerful and effective." NIV (James 5:16). Even when God didn't want to act, your prayer will set Him into action. And you can do all things because he strengthens you. (cc Phil. 4:13). Whenever you cry, heaven listens because you are a son of the kingdom. When Hezekiah received a prophecy from the Lord through the prophet Isaiah that he will die and not live. He prayed to the lord thus:

Hezekiah faced the wall and prayed to the Lord God. O Lord, remember, how I have walked before you blameless and with wholehearted devotion and dedication and have done what is right before your eyes. (Is: 38:3)

And immediately that decision was revisited. The Lord changed his mind because Hezekiah challenged him with his good works. Isaiah was sent again to tell him that he will no longer die. An additional fifteen years has been added to his life. A righteous man's prayer! He presented his righteousness and even though the decision had been taken that he will die, it was immediately changed. When you lift up your hands in prayer, what does the Lord see? Righteousness or iniquity? Learn from Hezekiah.

Rev. Fr. Anthony de Mello told a story of Narada, the Hindu Sage, who was on a pilgrimage to the temple of the Lord. He received hospitality one night in the house of a barren couple. Before he set out again, the man said to Narada, "You are going to worship the Lord. Tell him to give me a child".

Narada said to the Lord, "be merciful to that man and give him a child," the Lord replied, with an air of finality, "it is not in the destiny of that man to have children." So, Narada performed his devotions and went back home.

Five year later he was on pilgrimage again and was again given shelter by the hospitable couple. At this particular time, two little kids were playing at the door of the house. "Whose children are these? Said Narada.

"Mine", said the man. Narada was intrigued. And he continued, five years ago, when you left us, a Sannyasi came here to our town. We sheltered him for the night and the next day, before he left, he blessed my wife and me... and these are the fruit of his blessing."

When Narada got to the temple next day, he shouted from the forecourt, "Did you not tell me it was not in the destiny of that man to have children? He has two!" The Lord laughed aloud when he heard this. "That must be the doing of a Saint," he said. Saints have the power to change destiny!"

Saints have power to change destiny. This is exactly what happened at the wedding feast in Canaan when the mother of Jesus goes him to work a miracle before his destiny allowed it. Friends of God have the power to change the world. Situations bow before them. At their command, the impossible becomes possible. Join the train and you will tell the story.

CHAPTER THREE

BUILDING A PRAYER LIFE

WHY SHOULD WE PRAY?

What I have done in the last two chapters is to prepare you for what is to come, put your mind aright and to help you understand what prayer is and what it is not. Now is the time for you to begin praying. No amount of speculation about prayer will make you a prayer warrior unless you begin to pray. The only way out in a world of confusion like ours, where Satan has unleashed his venom with all its bitterness is to PRAY. If you don't pray, problems will kill you, or better put, Satan will turn you into pepper soup, obstacles will mess you up, and your life will be filled with stories of woes and failures. Our Lord warns.

Watch and pray, lest you enter into temptation. (Mat. 26:41).

Take heed, watch and pray; (Mark 13:33a)

Be alert and vigilant; because your enemy the devil is walking about like a roaring lion, searching for whom to devour. (1 Peter 5:8).

The greatest mistake people make is to wait till when obstacles have driven them to their knees before they begin to pray, crying, running up and down. Is it not better to begin before you are down? Establish that relationship with God now. Don't wait until problems push you to do so. If you are already down, rise up and start praying. The days are bad, wickedness is on the increase, diseases are everywhere even incurable ones, hunger, starvation, and war are devastating the world. There are so many evils in the world today and manipulations of devils and demonic agents. Everything is turning upside down and people are getting more and more confused. There are churches and ministries here and there, but most of them are not helping matters.

People get into there in search of solutions to their problems and they are duped with promises that never materialize. And even in extreme cases used for evil rituals. Wait! Don't get trapped. Don't get confused. There is only one way out: PRAY. Leonard Ravehill in his book "Why Revival Tarries" puts it this way:

There are complaints here and there about bad Governments, evils in the society, disease, and other satanic manipulations, yet alas, only a few of us can remember the last time we missed our bedtime for a night of waiting upon the Lord for a world-shaking revival.

When Christians pray, situations bow but when they sleep situations blow. A kneeling Christian never fails, but a non-praying one is abysmal of failure. Prayer is our only weapon of war. If you don't pray, no matter how you complain, obstacles will mess you up. Leonard Ravehill further speaks on this:

No man is greater than his prayer life. The pastor that is not praying is playing; the people who are not praying are straying. As poverty-stricken as the church is today in many things, she is most stricken here, in place of prayer. There are many organizers, but very few agonizers; many payers and players, no prayers; too many singers, small clingers; so many preachers, few wrestlers; much fears, little tears; much fashion, little passion: many interferes, very few intercessors; too many writers, but few fighters, failing here, we fail everywhere.

Who are those that conquer the world? They are those that understand the secret of going to God in Prayer. There, they draw strength and power to do exploits. They are bestowed with a marvelous charisma to command and control situations and the world. God governs the world but Prayer governs God (Pieta Prayer Book). Such souls rise at night and spend one hour or more in prayer; they observe total abstinence from food and drink one day a week; they diligently attend to all their obligations; and if duties permit, they attend Mass, receive Holy Communion, and daily spend an hour before the Blessed Sacrament. Gradually, these souls are purified, their defects disappear one after another, and virtues spring up.

Their possession and unions with God become more profound each day. (Immaculata Publication, 1974).

WE LEARN TO PRAY BY PRAYING

Dear reader, your desire to pray made you pick up this book. It is proof that the Holy Spirit dwells in you. David had a similar experience:

As a deer yearns for running streams, so I yearn for you, my God. I thirst for the Almighty God, the living and everlasting God; when shall I go to behold your face oh God?

But the desire alone is not enough if not followed by action. St Paul instructed Timothy to fan into flame the gifts of the Holy Spirit he received when he was laid hands upon. (See 2 Tim. 1:6). You need to stir the desire in you, which is the power of the Holy Spirit working through you, to action. Make a firm decision today to spend time with the Lord in prayer, even as you are reading this book. Stick to it. Pull yourself to carry it out. It may be difficult at the start, but as you advance, it will become easier. The difficulty or weakness you may experience in the course of your prayer is not because you are not willing to pray or because the Holy Spirit is not in you but because you have a willing spirit enveloped in weak flesh. The Bible says:

The spirit is very willing, but the flesh is so weak. (Mat. 26:41b).

Therefore, you must get the flesh, the weak body to obey the spirit. You must work on your flesh, your body, train it to obey your spirit. Doers get to the top of the oak tree by climbing it. Dreamers sit at the acorn. (J. Maurus). All your desire to pray will never be achieved unless you put it to action with considerable amount of discipline and determination. The truth is that a lot of people know the importance of prayer. They say it, they write it, they sing it, yet only very few can really pray, because it is one thing to know it and another to do it. Transform the will power in you into action and your life will never remain the same. As you will it, pray it out and it will be yours. Everything is possible for a man of prayer.

SPENDING A DAILY HOUR WITH THE LORD

The word of our Lord Jesus Christ on this is very clear "How is it that you three were not able to keep watch with me even for one hour?" (Mat. 26:40) Daily Hour with the Lord is not just a necessity but a prerequisite for Christian Living. The Apostle Peter even though he was willing to suffer with Christ unto death (And Peter spoke up and said to Jesus, "I will never leave you, even though all the rest do!") could not go an inch because he failed to understand this great secret – daily hour with the Lord.

I got involved in the Catholic Charismatic Renewal of Nigeria in 1993. As a beginner with an ardent desire and thirst for God. I tried to participate fully and actively in all activities of the movements; ranging from weekly prayer meetings to crusades and seminars. It was then that I first experienced the power in prayer and it dawned on me that prayers are not said for formality's sake as I used to do before, but the experience is real. Even though I have experienced the power in prayer then, I was still not a man of prayer until I encountered Rev. Fr. Stephen Njoku of the Upper Room Ministries in the following year. I began by reading his books especially. "The Key to Radical Prayer" and later I had the opportunity of encountering him face to face. It was through his instrumentality that I came to behold the importance of spending daily hour with the Lord. I began to do it. It wasn't easy the first time but as time went by, it became part of me. Indeed, it is an overwhelming experience. Today I sing of it and bear testimony of the Lord's goodness and His glorious encounter. Part of it is what you are reading now. Alleluia!

The key to our Lord's success lies in his prayer life. Jesus would spend the whole night in prayer. (See Luke 6:12). This is a model for all Christians. If you want to do the great or even greater works of the kingdom as Jesus did, then you must maintain a personal daily prayer, at least an hour with him. If you want to walk above human problems and difficulties, then you must spend an hour with him. If you share this holy thought of getting to heaven hereafter, then stay with him daily.

It is in those hours that you will draw strength to do exploits, command and control situations. This is not praying when problems and obstacles have driven you to do so but maintaining a constant communion with God. The Saints understood this great secret of success and embraced it. St. Francis used to spend whole nights praying before the Blessed Sacrament, and often people used to see a light shining from his face, lighting up the whole church. When a man asked him. "What do you do in the church at night?" He answered: What does a man dying of thirst do when he finds water? I drink in Jesus. I pray. I adore. I love. Archbishop Fulton Sheen made a vow during his priestly ordination to spend at least an hour every day in private adoration before the Holy Eucharist and he grew to be the most influential American Bishop. A Notebook on the Devil and Exorcism comments on this thus: "It is possible for everyone to lead a life which eventually would dispose one for the grace of full possession by the Holy Spirit. It is not hard to spend an hour every night in prayer. People in the world spend much more than one hour, often entire nights in drinking, dancing, at card table or in the theatre. Christ and his Apostles practiced the nightly prayer; the Blessed Mother and Holy Women rose at midnight for prayer; the Saints practiced this devotion. In the silence of the night, undisturbed by the world, their souls are united to God. Night is the time when most of the crimes are committed. Reparation is made by most of the chosen ones. During the day, if we would only give to prayer the time, which is otherwise wasted, we would all become great saints. Prayer makes saints."

Map out at least one hour within the 24hours of a day to spend with the Lord Jesus in personal prayer. When I say personal prayer. I mean personal prayer, a time you will be alone with God. This is what is called quiet time. (I will come back to it). This is different from your fellowship time or group worship. It should be a time set aside and you must not allow your duties to interfere with it. Therefore, choose a time that is most suitable. Spiritual writers have often recommend at the middle of the night when the world is cool and still or at the break of the dawn before the busy day begins. This time helps us to pray without much distraction. In any case, you are free to choose a better time for yourself, but don't push it to a time that you are weak and tired from day's activities. It may be very difficult for you to proceed this time. Forcing yourself to continue under such heavy conditions may be endangering your health. If you must choose evening, consider observing your quiet time before dinner. Experience has shown that after meal, during the process of digestion that we tend to feel sleepy. If you can set out time to have your quiet time during the day, better. But you must be careful not to allow the day's distractions and worries take over the prayer time. Finally, whichever time you choose, try to make it, as much as you can, permanent and stick to it. Choose a quiet place: in the church, in your room, at a cool and quiet spot or else, go into the internal recess of your heart.

HOW TO DEAL WITH THE WEAK FLESH

A close friend of mine during my university days called me one day and said "Humphrey, it is not that I don't understand what you are saying, but each time, I try to live as you are living, I find it difficult, too difficult to do. I then concluded that it is not my gift." He turned to me and said "it is your gift, continue to live in it, as long as I don't steal, God understands." My friend is the type that lives a reckless and licentious life. He made the above statement because I have always taken time to exhort him to accept Christ and change his rotten behaviour. Immediately he finished speaking I closed my eyes to remember St. Paul lament of the same problem in Romans chapter seven, "I do not understand what I do; for I don't do what I would like to do, but instead I do what I hate." (Rom. 7:15 GNB). But the difference here is that St. Paul didn't bow for he said: who will deliver me from this body that is taking me to death, thanks to God, who does this through our Lord Jesus Christ. St. Paul lifted up his eyes and saw a solution, but my friend bowed and accepted defeat. The impossible becomes possible when we look beyond our mortal body to behold the Spirit that gives the body life.

Our Lord Jesus knows that weak we are. That is why he says "I will send you an Advocate, the Spirit of the living God. The Holy Spirit comes to aid us in our weakness: He fills us with power to overcome the flesh. The scripture says:

In the same way, the Spirit too comes to the aid of your weakness; for we do not know how to pray as we ought, but the Spirit itself intercedes with inexpressible groanings. (Rom. 8:26).

This is what the Spirit of God does for us. The Lord instructed the disciple not to leave the Upper Room until the Spirit comes and when the Spirit came, those timid and shy fishermen were transformed into vibrant and glorious instrument in the hands of the Lord. The apostles who couldn't drive out mute spirit from a boy in Mark chapter 9, were not only instruments of miracles in the Acts of the Apostles after Pentecost but even the sick were placed on roadsides so that their shadows might fall on them. (See Acts 5:15). Peter who denied Jesus before a slave girl was bold enough not only to face the Jewish council but preached Jesus to them (See Acts 2). The Apostle who couldn't spend an hour with Jesus in Gethsemane prayed Peter out of Prison in such a manner that left the soldiers in utter confusion. This is the work of the Spirit. So, open up to the Spirit of God so that He will transform you. Hunger and thirst for the Holy Spirit. Pray for it. Wait for it. Allow him to transform you. This is the first stage.

As you cannot pray well without the Holy Spirit, so also the Holy Spirit cannot transform your life without your compliance. A child called out to his father one day "Daddy, carry me" and his father called out "Johnny give me your hand." The scriptures says, "the Spirit too comes to the aid of our weakness". The word "aid" means, "to assist." That means that the Spirit does not just do it for us but assists us in doing it. No wonder St. Paul exhorted Timothy to fan into flame the gift of the Holy Spirit he received when he was laid hand upon. (See 2 Tim. 1:6). The Spirit is already in him to assist him work it out, but he has to stand up. If he doesn't, the fire of the Spirit in him will be quenched. St. Paul warned, "Do not quench the Spirit." (1 Thess. 5:19). I am taking time to emphasize this because many Christians, I came to notice, backslide after the baptism of the Holy Spirit because they think that the Holy Spirit does everything without their contribution. This is wrong. The truth is that the Spirit empowers us and we can use this power or waste it. St Bernard of Clairvaux exhorts, "gird your loins, put aside idleness, grasp the mettle, and do some hard work." Therefore, another important stage in this exercise is to train your body to obey the Spirit. St. Paul told Timothy in first Timothy 4:7b-10:

Exercise yourself for godliness, for, while physical training has limited value, godliness is valuable in every respect, since it holds a promise of life both for the present and for the future.

This saying is trustworthy and deserves full acceptance.

For this we toil and struggle, because we have set our hope on the living God, who is the saviour of all, especially of those who believe."

Those who are engaged in sports undertake a lot of practice and training to keep themselves fit for the game. Heavy weight lifters take time to practice, select their meals and guard against whatever that will cause loss of weight. This is because they have an eye on their rewards, the wreath of victory that will be given to them at the end. Donald was to represent his school in an athletic competition. He practices six hours daily, three in the morning, three in the evening and allows nothing come in between. He takes time to select his meal: he goes for chips when he should have taken burger, water instead of malts and fruits instead of meat. He watches himself very carefully to avoid every cause of failure. On the day of the game he matched out with confidence. At the sound of the gun, he took off, moving with the speed of the air. Along the way he had dislocation on his ankle joint. He jumped and leaped in great pains, moved on with much determination and vigour. Pushing a little further, he was at the finishing line. Donald has won a gold medal. The crowd applauded him; the crowd cheered him – ah the noise was so much. Cries of victory soared the air. The joy was enormous. His Rector couldn't help dancing in the field uncontrollably. Donald has succeeded in winning a gold medal.

No one thought of the deep pain, the strenuous exercise, the poor meal, the long training hours and all what he went through. No, the only important thing was that he had won a gold medal. Only Donald knew the Secret. Genius is one-percent inspiration but ninety-nine percent perspiration. He understood this.

Donald won a wreath – true, but this is only one that will wither. St. Paul would tell us that ours lasts forever. We are working for a crown that lasts forever. Spiritual exercise holds a promise both for the present and the future. Therefore, beloved, undertake enough spiritual exercises to overcome the weight of your body and sour in the Spirit. The Master

Praised the servant in Luke chapter 16:3-8 for his wisdom with these words: "the children of this world are more prudent in dealing with their own generation than are the children of light".

If Donald can spend such time and energy working for an earthly reward; if he can pay such sacrifices for a wreath that withers, how much more ours that last forever, and has a better promise both for present and future. Plan your day well; spend time in prayer; train your body; move on even in pains of trials and persecution with determination and vigor. The Holy Spirit is there to empower you. Do it a little more and the glory will be yours.

Spiritual exercises are those activities that mortify the flesh and liberate the soul and slacken it not whenever it wants from attaining the heavenly glories. Beloved, if you eat whenever you feel like eating, you will never be a good prayer warrior for nothing weighs down the souls like superfluity of food and gluttony. Our Lord warns "Be careful, or your hearts will be weighed down with dissipation, drunkenness and the anxieties of life" (Lk. 21:34). Take a little fast to teach your flesh that man does not live by bread alone. In the same way, if you sleep whenever you feel like sleeping you will not be prayerful, for too much sleeping hinders the soul and weakens the body and makes it vulnerable to temptation. While men were sleeping, the enemy came and sowed tears among the wheat and left. (Matt. 13:25 NKJ). Practice self-denial to prepare your souls for greater communion with God. Self-denial enriches the souls. St Paul says:

I keep disciplining my body to bring it into control, least, when I have ministered to others, I myself should become disqualified. (1 Cor. 9:27).

Discipline the senses and subject them under strict obedience. Let the eyes not look at everything it sees. Give not your ear to every talk that passes. Regulate what the tongue utters. And above all do not overload the soul with inordinate passion such as sexual desires, perilous amusement, worldly vanity and the likes. These desires are only dangerous and only distract and weary the heart.

Beloved, remember these virtues may not be easy to acquire, that's the more reason why you should take time to practice it. Be conscious of them and struggle to acquire them, diligently work for it and it will be yours. May the Lord guide you in this.

MORTIFICATION OPENS THE WAY

Beloved, I want to talk about mortification now in details. The truth is that without mortification we will find it difficult to pray. Since our body will continue to draw us down, subjecting it under total control opens the way for an ardent prayer experience. Mortification comes from the word "to mortify" which means to subdue the bodily desires and passions. By way of mortification, we discipline the body and subject it into total obedience to the soul, for the flesh has desires against the spirit, and the Spirit against flesh; these are opposed to each other, so that you may not do want you want (Galations 5:17). We mortify our body by way of fasting and abstinence. "If you are not able to fast, do well to observe some abstinence beyond what is enjoined by the Church, for in addition to ordinary benefits of fasting, namely, lifting up the mind, subduing the flesh, strengthening virtue, and earning an eternal recompense, it is a great matter to be able to command our tastes and inclinations, and keep the flesh and its appetites subject to the law of the spirit (St. Francis De Sales, 1923). We can fast from food, drinks and sensual pleasures. We can fast wholly from food and drinks or partially from those items of food or drink that appeal more to our sense for instance meat and wine. Another excellent way is to deny ourselves of those pleasure that tend to lead us to excessive relaxation, useless enjoyment and make us prone to temptation like ling watching of television or surfing of web, extravagant parties, excessive use of cosmetics and costly make up, idle discussions and the likes. But in all these things care must be taken so that the fasting or denial will not be just ordinary external gestures, born out of selfish interest and vain glory. Such act instead of enriching the soul destroy it. Our Lord Jesus condemned the Pharisees for this, even though he fasted two times a week, his prayer was not answered because he was full of pride. (cf. Luke 18:9-14). Our fasting should be borne out of real internal desire to please God. It should dispose more of us to practice acts of charity, which will open us to the love of God and make our prayer fervent. It is said that Jacinta, Francisco and Lucia, the young Fatima visionaries, as a kind of fact used to throw their food away instead of taking them, but later repented of this and start sharing it with the hungry since it pleases the Lord to do so than throwing it away. Our fast should dispose us more to do good to our neighbours and serve God better.

Beloved, I must warn that in everything, you do, do it with moderation. Doctors always advise that taking overdose of any drug destroys the body system instead of healing it. On the other hand, not taking the drug at all is even more dangerous. The best is to stick to direction and prescription. The same can be said of fasting. Without fasting prayerful life becomes very difficult, but excessive fasting easily leads into indulgence and luxury. St. Francis de Sales says that we are exposed to temptation when the body is over indulged and when it is subdued; for us the one makes it easy and indolent, so the other makes it low and despondent; and just as we cannot control it when it is over-fed, neither can it serve us when it is under-fed. The best is always to take it gradually, little by little with steady effort and by the Grace of God, one will grow into a spiritual giant like St. Francis of Assisi who fasted for 40 days after the example of our Lord Jesus.

Finally, whichever way you choose to mortify your flesh, I advise, in the words of St. John Chrysostom, that the right disposition behind a fact is as critical as the amount of prayer a person undertook. Your fast should dispose you to pray well. It should bring you to an intimate union with God and propel you to virtue otherwise it will just be starving.

A SHORT PLAN FOR YOUR QUIET TIME

Beloved, for your quiet time I recommend mental prayer, the prayer of the heart. It is also called Mind prayer, a heart to heart conversation with God. This is a perfect way of praying. I know you are used to vocal prayer, saying prayer made by another person or patterning your prayer after the words of your minister or others in your fellowship or prayer meetings, but in mental prayer, you talk to God from your heart. "There was an old priest who used to spend hours in the church at night, praying in the dark. He was asked, Padre, how do your pray there all alone at night? He answered, I think of Him looking back at me. I say nothing. I feel Him with my heart. When my mind wanders, I say His Holy Name a few times to bring it back. That's all.' And that was prayer without words. A holy woman wrote, 'I think I never pray so well as when I sit down quietly at home, and open my heart to

Jesus without saying anything, and let Him look into it. Then his love flows in, healing and consoling." (Malachy Cullen, 1983). This doesn't mean that you should stop vocal prayer – no, but mental prayer is always the best.

Nothing illumines the soul and exposes it to the warmth of God's love and healing power like mental prayer. It draws us closer to God and makes our heart beats in one with him. In mental prayer, we dwell in him, who alone is the reason for our existence, the sure dwelling of our soul. We gaze at him who is the true happiness, joy and peace of our soul. Our soul yearns for him, even though, we try to fill it with worldly vanities, its wounds will never be healed unless it embraces its creator, whom alone can satisfy it. St. Augustine says "You have made us for yourself, O Lord, and our hearts are restless till they rest in you." God is the utmost need of our soul. And mental prayer makes our soul the true abode of God. The Psalmist says: As the deer yearns for streams of living water, so my soul yearns for you, O Lord my God. My whole soul yearns for God, for the living God. When can I go and meet with God? (Ps. 42:1-2). Mental prayers present you before God as you are, and help to bridge that gap that separates you from God. David cried out: search me, O Lord God, and see my heart; test me and know my deep thoughts. See if there is any evil way in me, and lead me in the life everlasting. In this kind of prayer you dwell alone with God, savouring the riches of his goodness. You enjoy the joy of being in his presence just as lovers do in the presence of each other. In fact, beloved if you want to know the joy of the saints, then you must practice mental prayer.

I am now going to present to you a short plan for mental prayer to guide you. I know you may not have been practicing it because it seems difficult, but this simple way handed over to us by the saints will help simplify it. Make it part of you. Remember to find a quiet corner either in your house or your office or better still in the church that will offer you the peace and tranquility you need and help avoid disturbance of friends, colleagues and family members. I will now present these steps in five stages.

Stage one: Scripture Reading.

As you are about to begin your mental prayer with Bible reading, recognize that you are in the presence of God and that God is everywhere. As birds, no matter where they fly to will always meet air, so also, no matter where we go, we will always be in the presence of God, for it is in him we live, move and have our whole being. Ask God to help you behold this truth and to pray. Then open the Bible and begin to read. I recommend that you read from the Gospels, for example, the crucifixion of our Lord Jesus Christ. (John 16:16 – 42). Read it once, read twice, read in between line and allow it to sink into you. You can also take your reading from the Church liturgical calendar. There are many good devotionals to guide you.

Stage two: Imagination

Imagine our Lord Jesus Christ as real and present, which actually is the truth, even though physically you cannot see him. Close your eyes and try to picture the scene from the Gospel you read, in this case, where our Lord Jesus is being nailed to the cross. A conversation transpired between a Guru and an atheist, and the atheist asked him "why is it that you are so sure that you can convince me that there is God?" And the Guru answered, "Because even now, I see Him (God) more clearly than I see you" Great! That is the conviction that makes a Saint. Faith in action; making those eternal truths real and actual. Blind Bartimaeus, even though he was blind, pictured Jesus in his imagination, believed in his heart and cried out for help and he was healed. The Lord says blessed are those who did not (physically) see and believed. In the spirit, we continue to see Jesus and this is always true. Vividly represent, by the aid of the imagination, the mystery on which you are about to mediate as though it were going on before your very eyes. In this instance, picture our Lord Jesus being nailed to the cross and allow the imagination to illumine your heart.

Third Stage: Meditation

The act of imagination is followed by an act of understanding, which is meditation. Now begin to reflect on the spiritual reading – the passion of Christ. As the last stage helped you to picture yourself in Calvary, think of why and how Jesus is being nailed on the cross and for whom he is suffering for. St. Francis de Sale tells us that the difference between mediation and study or any other processes of thought, is that the later have not viture and love of God for their end, for their object is temporal, such as acquisition of knowledge, for purpose of discussion, composition etc. Mediation fills our soul with love of God and our neighbours and great zeal and desire for heavenly things. Reflection on these truths of our faith, passion of Christ in this instance, will induce a deep thought, sorrow and pity in you and ignite a fire of God's love as you mediate on the lamb that was scourged and killed that you might live. Remember, if not for Jesus we would have wasted away. A criminal who was previously condemned to death, was surprised to receive the news that he has been discharged and acquitted. When he inquired what happened he was told that somebody offered to pay his price. And he exclaimed "Show me the person and I will live the rest of my life for him." Jesus offered his life that you might live. He was bruised for our iniquity.

Stage Four: Conversation

I know you are moved to talk to Jesus, don't hesitate. Go on talk to him in your own words. With deep sorrow, tell Jesus that you are sorry for your sin. Speak to him from your heart. Let your heart beat for him. Let Jesus know that you love him. He is just there before you, looking back to you with love. Assure him of your love and faithfulness. Open your heart for him, adore him. Talk to him…. Tell Jesus about your problems and that of your neighbors.

This is what is called a heart to heart conversation with God, in our mind – conversation without words. This is what is called mind prayer. Have you ever been in the presence of the one you love? How do you feel? His or her presence just makes you happy, even when you are not talking to each other. At times you may just look at each other and your eyes and hearts will communicate a message that words cannot explain. In mental prayers, we touch our heart with the heart of Jesus, we communicate, we talk, we enjoy, and we relax in each other.

Stage Five:　　　　Silence

This is the height of mental prayer. At this stage you remain just silent before God, with your mind fixed on him – no talking. You are just looking at him and he is looking back at you. In silent adoration, you dwell in his presence, savouring the joy of his company. Mother Teresa of Calcutta says that silence is the root of our union with God. This is not the time to ask or demand from the Lord or mediate or sing but just to adore him with silence. The God says: Be still, and you will know that I am God. (Ps. 46:10). Try to maintain an internal peace and inward quietness. If your mind wanders, bring it back by repeating some aspirations (I will explain this later) and continue to adore him with silence. Stay on. I recommend that you spend just one hour, for now, in your quiet time. Don't go beyond that, unless your spiritual director advises otherwise. Beginners may not be able to spend up to one hour at the beginning. Let it this not worry you. Begin with what you can and gradually grow in it.

Yes, this may be difficult at the start of it, but don't be discouraged for nothing good comes easy. Hold on to it, with time it will become part of you. A little child trying to learn how to ride a bicycle, always finds it difficult at the start, but perseverance gives him success. Someone expressed this beautiful thought: "walk on! To talk with God, no breath is lost. Talk on! To walk with God, no strength is lost. Walk on! To wait on God, no time is lost. Walk on!" He who interrupts the course of his spiritual exercise and prayer, St. John of the cross would say, is like a man who allows a bird to escape from his hand; he can hardly catch it. As a young student, when I first started practicing waking up to read in the night, I always found in difficult, very difficult that at times I wake up, it seems as if I developed malaria fever over night. But as I pressed on, it became part of me that I don't even need an alarm clock or someone to wake me up. This taught me a great lesson and was a great lesson to me when I began quiet time. St. Vincent de Paul crowned it up by saying that human nature grows tired of always doing the same thing, and it is God's will that this should be so because of the opportunity of practicing two great virtues. The first is perseverance, which will bring us to our goal. The other is steadfastness, which overcomes the difficulties on the way. Our Lord told us to always pray continually and never lose faith (Luke 18:1).

CENTERING PRAYER

St. Francis de Sales told Philothea, from time to time then, gather your spirit into the solitude of your heart, where, separate from all men, you can lay open your soul and speak face to face with God. "In centering prayer, we retire into our heart, which is the abode of God, maintain an inward quietness, and worship God in utmost silence. The Bible says: Do you not understand that your body is the temple of the Holy Spirit (1 Cor. 6:19). God lives in our heart. The format is very simple. Desert Fathers teaches that first of all we find for ourselves a quiet corner, retire into our heart in solitude, shut the door of our heart from worries and distractions, and fix our minds on God. Choose a position most suitable for you that will help you relax very well, possibly, sitting down. Take a deep breath, in and out for about ten times very slowly. This relaxes your nerve and helps you maintain an inward quietness. At this time begin to call, with deep calm, the Holy name of Jesus softly. Continue repeating the name for few minutes, and gently allow it to die out quietly. Then silence, utmost silence. No Words! At this time, you are in the presence of the most high God. Just remain quiet before him. No talking, no mediation, just relax, with your heart continually fixed on Jesus, listening. If you are distracted take deep breath a few times again and repeat some aspiration.

This will bring back your mind and refocus you in his presence.   You can spend an hour or less in this prayer, but don't watch the clock, allow the Holy Spirit to lead the way. This means that you must find for yourself a better time for this prayer, so that it will not clash with your duty.

ASPIRATION AND EJACULATORY PRAYER

Beloved, by the use of aspirations and ejaculatory prayers, we can maintain a continuous and constant relationship with God throughout the day. Just like fishes don't survive outside water, in the same way we can't survive outside God. The Scripture holds that "as longs Moses held up his hands, the Israelites were winning, but whenever he lowered his hands, the Amalekites were winning. (See Exodus 17:11). As long as we keep on praying, we will keep on winning, but when we stop praying, the enemy will keep on winning. We need to maintain a constant union with God so that the enemy will be destroyed forever. To achieve this, therefore, our prayers should not only be limited to Sunday worship, weekly fellowship or even morning and evening prayers alone but we should always rise to God in prayers in and out of seasons.

St. Paul says "pray in the Spirit on all occasions with all kinds of prayers and requests." As we go about our daily businesses, we should frequently turn our mind to God in constant invocation of his holy name. This keeps us always connected. Lovers talk of each other all the time. Even when they are not together, the thought of each other never fades from their memory. This is because it illuminates their heart and calms their tension. In the same way, but much more than that, if we truly love God, we should be able to turn our mind back to him a thousand times, fix it constantly on him adoring and invoking his aid throughout the day. This will keep us constantly in his presence.

We achieve this by the use of those short prayers and invocations of His holy name that illuminate the heart, such as those found in the Psalm of David, in the Gospel and the spiritual collections of the Saints. This is called Aspirations and Ejaculatory prayers because by the use of this prayer we long for (aspire) and retire in God that so loves us. Such prayers, St. Francis de Sales exhorts, may be interwoven with our businesses and occupations without hindering them in the slightest degree. Instead of hindering our work, It even helps us to do better.

I am now going to give you a list of these aspirations to help you get started, but try to find that which best suits your hearts; you are by no means restricted to these ones. Now here is the list: My Lord and my God; Jesus I love you; Jesus my Lord; Jesus, son of David have mercy on me; Oh great God; Create a pure heart in me Oh God; Bless me Lord; Lord let me see your glory; I adore you Jesus; The Lion from the tribe of Judea; Jesus meek and humble of heart, make my heart like unto thine; I am healed; Jesus I love you with all my heart etc.

As you go through this list and others you will find in the scriptures, you will find that which suits you best. Please use it and make it your own. These aspirations can be best said following the rhythm of heart beats or body movements. Also, as Psychologists teach, repeating these aspirations several times help register it in our memory. That is why teachers often make children to repeat new words over and over again at a time, even make song with it. At the time I started, I took time to study my walking steps and chose aspiration that goes in line with it. As I raise my leg up and down. I recite: my Lord and my God, within my heart. That is when one leg is up, I say "My Lord", when it is down, I complete it "My God". If I walk fast, I change it to Jesus, Jesus, Jesus, Jesus I love you. It so became part of me that sometimes, I sing this unconsciously. When I am in a vehicle, at work or at rest, I change it to something else. Aspiration keep us connected and, in his presence, always; practice it.

Another good use of aspiration is to fight distractions during prayer, especially during quiet time. If distractions come as you plunge into His presence, during your quiet time, fight it by repeating some aspirations or ejaculatory prayer. Repeat it a few times and plunge back into his presence. This will keep you focused. I will teach you more about distraction in the following chapters. Let this help you get started.

CHAPTER FOUR

PRAYER AND SPIRITUAL GROWTH

Your prayer power depends on your stage in the spiritual ladder. The more you press on to spiritual maturity the more closely you get to God and the more efficacious your prayer becomes. A spiritual giant demonstrates a higher spiritual exercise while the prayer of a spiritual baby reflects his stage. The Apostles were unable to cast out a demon from a boy in Mark Chapter nine, even though they used the same words Jesus uses and did it also in Jesus way, but they lacked the power with which Jesus operates. But in Acts of the Apostles, the same Apostles who couldn't cast out demons were set vibrant and on Holy Ghost fire after they had passed through three years of thorough training under the Master Jesus. The Apostles who couldn't pray for even one hour in Matthew chapter 26 verse 40, prayed to the point that the house they were staying began to shake (See Acts 4:31). The healing they couldn't perform with all their prayers in Mark Chapter 9 began to happen to such a point that even their shadows also caused miracles to happen. (See Acts 5:15) Your prayer efficacy is not determined at all by your choice of words or prayer book but by your spiritual height. The style that is unproductive in the hands of a spiritual infant may be a powerful tool in the hands of a Saint. It all depends on how close you are to God and how genuine and right is your relationship with Him.

Growth means increase. It is a process every living being passes through. By Spiritual Growth, we mean growth in Holiness; an advancement towards Christian maturity – a stable Christian life. As we grow physically so also, we grow spiritually. Conversion and repentance mark the beginning of heavenly journey but not all that is needed for it. Repentance fills the soul with a kind of joy and happiness that is beyond understanding. This is the Glory of a new life in Christ. This is a result of the immense treasure and riches and Glory one came to behold in Christ. This could make one spend hours in prayers without getting tired. This could make one carry out Church activities without complaints. This could bring one closer to God and make one walk in his presence. This is the condition Peter, James and John, found themselves, when our Lord Jesus Christ called them, the Bible says they left everything – their father, their boat, their net and followed him. Peter (with James and John) also experienced such Glory again on Mount Olivet during Transfiguration that he wants to remain there forever. These joys and glories of repentance helps one get started but if not nurtured to maturity it dies off. It is not a permanent state.

The person who received the seed that dropped on rocky ground is the man who hears God's word and immediately receives it with joy. But because he has no root, he lasts only a little while. When problem or persecution comes due to of the word, he immediately falls away. (Matt. 13: 20 – 21)

It is only there to launch you to a greater Glory which you can get by consolidation your effort and pressing on to maturity. When Nathaniel encountered Jesus, his joy was excessive but Jesus told him that it is just beginning for he is even going to see greater glory.

(cfJohn 1:50). There are natural traits and inclinations in you that you need to deal with and subject it under total control otherwise it will crop up and strangle the good fruits planted in you. Out of these traits, the main one is temperament, which exacts the greatest influence on human behaviour. Temperament is the combination of traits we inherited from our parents. It is the combination of unborn traits that subconsciously affect man's behaviour. The Bible called it many names like the hidden man, the natural man, the flesh, sinful nature and so on. If not controlled, the negative influence of temperament can make a Christian behave more like an unbeliever. In spite of the Glory and Power St Paul encountered on the road to Damascus, he still had to fight this flesh and subject it under control.

I do not understand what I do. For the things I desire to do I don't do, but the things I hate I do. (cf. Romans 7:15).

In his Epistle to the Galatians, St Paul confessed of his victory over the flesh, the sinful nature that is dragging him to hell.

I am crucified with Christ Jesus and therefore, I no longer live, but Christ Jesus lives in me. This very life I live in the body, I live by faith in Christ, Son of God, who loved me so much and gave life for me. (cf. Gal. 2: 20)

This is the Glory of the Saints, a mature Christian Life. Christ lives, works and it made manifest through all the works of the Saints. This is a call to all Christians. St Paul emphasized this in all his teachings. In his Letter to the Galatians St Paul scolded the Galatians for starting in the Spirit and ending in the flesh.

Are you so stupid? After starting in the Spirit, are you now ending it in the flesh? (cf. Gal. 3:3)

He further distinguished the stages in Spiritual Growth as spiritual baby that takes milk and matured Christian that takes solid food.

I gave you milk, and not solid food, because you were not able to take it. Indeed, you are still not able, even now, or you are still of the flesh. When there is jealousy and opposition in your midst, are you not dwelling in the flesh, and behaving in a mere human way? (Cf. 1 Cor. 3: 2-3).

The writer of Hebrews puts this even in a clearer term:

Every person who feeds on milk lacks experience of the word of righteousness, for he is still a child. But the solid food is for the mature ones, for those whose abilities are trained by constant practice to distinguish between good and evil. So, let us keep behind us the basic teaching about Christ Jesus and advance to full maturity, without laying the foundation from the beginning again: repentance from dead works and faith in God almighty (cf. Heb. 5:13 – 6:1).

In repentance, you are endowed with Divine Grace to enable you develop into a matured Soldier of Christ. It is then your obligation and duty to press on to maturity without allowing anything to draw you back. If you don't do this, the inborn traits and influence of the environment will quench the fire of the Spirit in you. St Paul told Timothy "to fan into flame the gift of God, which is in you through the laying on of my hands." (2 Timothy 1:6). In Timothy Chapter 4: 7 & 8, St Paul recommended Spiritual training as way of growing to maturity, thereby going beyond the basic training and moving to something higher and Glorious.

.... Train yourself in godliness, for, while physical exercise is of little value, godliness is valuable in every aspect, since it holds a promise of blessed life both for the present life and for the future.

Let us now examine in detail the various steps towards Spiritual maturity.

According to the teachings of the Church, I present below four elements which stand out prominently on how the faithful who are willing may grow in perfection and, with God's help, rise even to the heights of sanctity:

1.   DEEP AWARENESS OF THE PLAN OF GOD

The Almighty God created us to worship, reverence, and serve him, and through this means to save his life. Other things on earth are created for man to assist him in attaining this very end for which he is created. Hence, man is to make use of them in as much as they help him in the attainment of his end, and he must rid himself of them in as much as they prove to be a hindrance to him. (Hardon John, Catholic Catechism). A deep awareness of this plan of God for man: that you are created to serve and worship God here on earth in order to dwell with him eternally in heaven is a first stage of a deep spiritual growth. This must come to bear deeply on your consciousness. It is only and only when this is done that you will begin to look beyond the earth to behold heaven, the inheritance of the Saints. Again, this will help you to understand that you are only but a pilgrim on earth. All the glories of this world are like streams of water along the roadside. It helps the pilgrim keep going when he drinks and make the right use of it, but if he gets entangled with it, it draws him back and distracts him from his journey. All the glories of this world are transitory, they will all perish but one who possesses God lives forever. Only the one who understands this is wise. Our Lord Jesus Christ says: What will it profit a man if he gains the whole world, and forfeits his very soul? Or what will one pay in replacement for his soul?

J. Maurus told this story of an old man who at the point of death called his son, Robert to his Bedside. When he arrived, the man said with a radiant smile: "Robert, I am so glad you have come. There is something I want to tell you. When you decided to become a monk, I did all I could to make you change your mind. That was wrong. And for that I am heartily sorry now" There was a pause. Then fixing his tired eyes on his son, he said quickly: "Robert, I see so clearly now that there is only one mistake that one can make in life." Robert immediately asked what that mistake might be. With final struggle for breath to get out the words, his father said: "The only mistake that one can make in this life, my son is Not To Be A Saint."

When you live your daily life bearing in mind the plan and purpose of your creation, it makes you go through life living for heaven. There is nothing that ensnares the soul of a righteous man like the pleasures and glories of the world, even Jesus himself was tempted by Satan on this, (See Mat 4) but being fully aware of his mission on earth, Jesus conquered him. Use earthly things to support life, just like traveler's cake but never get entangled with it. Jesus says:

If your hand will cause you to commit sin, cut it off. It is better for you to go into heaven with one hand than with two hands to go into hell fire, where the fire does not go out. And you to go into heaven crippled than to have two feet and be cast into hell fire.

if your eye makes you to sin, pluck it out. For It is better for to enter the kingdom of heaven with one eye than to have both eyes and be thrown into hell fire, A place where their maggot dies not, and the ravaging fire is not extinguished. (Mark 9:45 - 49).

Awareness came from the word "Aware" which means, "to be conscious of". A discovery in psychotherapy holds that as an individual becomes more aware of all aspect of his experiences, he is increasingly likely to act in a manner we would term socialized. In this way if one understands and becomes fully aware; fully conscious of the reasons for his creation; the plan of God for him, his mission here on earth, he is more likely to be a Saint. Yes, this is true because only then will he appreciate the Creator and seek and struggle to behold him. Soldiers who get entangled with sensual pleasures or other trivial things in an enemy territory are only those who are not conscious of their mission. Awareness is to be continually present; to be totally there each moment; to be so absorbed with a fact that you are ceaselessly aware (conscious) of it. Therefore, let this Divine purpose for your life be permanently impressed on your mind and be ever fresh in your memory as you go about your daily duty and in all that you do, believe it and let it guide all your action.

2.   SELF-KNOWLEDGE

The Greek philosopher Epictetus said: "No man is free who is not a master of himself." Spiritual Growth begins with the realization of God's plan and purpose for one's life, but this is not all. One cannot seriously live a holy life without total knowledge of "one's sinfulness and weakness, as well as of virtue and strength" (The Catholic Catechism).

A thorough understand of one's limitations and capabilities will help one full control and mastery of his actions. Peter presumed his loyalty to Christ. He told Christ: "Lord, I am ready to go to prison and to death." (Lk.22:33) But thereafter, Peter finds himself failing again and again to the point that he denied his master. Peter thought he had the power to do it and was determined to do it, but there seems to be an internal force in him, which he was not aware of that seems to control his actions. This is the same problem, St. Paul complained of in Roman Chapter 7. Therefore, a good mastery of oneself is an indispensable tool toward perfection.

Self – Knowledge can be acquired through sound appraisal and deep study of one's behaviors and actions. This will help reveal one's weakness and strength. Two things control man's behaviour: Nature and Nurture. Nature is the inborn trait that we inherited from our parents. This is what is called temperament as we defined earlier. Nurture is the training, education and the influence of the environment. One has to listen, study and examine with open body, soul and spirit the influence of these two factors. Take time to examine your actions carefully and expose it to the teachings of Christ.

Jesus said:

"What makes a man unclean is what comes out of him. Evil thoughts, murder, deceit, arrogance, fornication, adultery, malice, slander, envy, stealing, greed, lewdness, folly, fall come from within out of men's hearts. These all evils habits come from inside of men and make him very unclean (Mark 7:20 – 23).

What causes fights and quarrels among you? Do they not come from your inner desires that battle inside of you? (James 4:1).

You are still worldly. Are you not still worldly, since jealousy and quarreling exist among you? Are you not acting like mere men? (1 Cor 3:3).

Remember what we taught, as regard your former life pattern, to cast out your old life, which is corrupted heavily by its evil desires and be made anew by the renewal of your minds; so that you can put on the new life, created to be like God Almighty in true holiness and righteousness. (Eph. 4:22-24).

Anyone who comes to me and does not hate his mother and father, his spouse and children, his sisters and brothers -- true, even his own very life- - he cannot be my disciple. And anyone who dose not carry his cross and follow me cannot be my disciple. lets suppose that one of you wants to build a house. Will he not sit down first and check the cost to confirm if he has good enough money to complete project? (Lk 14: 26-28 NIV)

Why is it that you are not able to keep most of your resolutions? Is there anything that stands between you and God either corporal or psychic? How ready are you to surrender these things to embrace God? Do you have inordinate attachment to anything created? How open is your heart to your neighbors? Why is it that your relationship with your neighbors suffers? Are you really responsible? Don't just wave it away, think. Think about it. Are you sure you are not responsible? Is there something in you that seems to go out of control most a times? What is it? Don't you know? Settle down and think about it you will find out. Are you easily irritated? What is the cause? Do you find yourself inclined to certain behavior? Have you thought about it? During those hours you are alone, what kind of thought do fill you mind. Does it have the love of God and neighbours at its centre or is full of selfishness. This is very important because your actions follow the rhythm of your heart, the thoughts on your minds. Sound appraisal done in spirit of humility no matter what cost to pride and complacency, or to sloth and natural timidity, has power of exposing the *real you to you*. Men, most times justify their action but it is only he who is humble enough to appraise his actions under the gentle love of the Holy Spirit will fully gain a mastery of his self. Remember that the Lord God does not see as men see; for men look at the physical appearance, but God looks at the heart. "(1 Sam. 16:7).

According to Tim Lahaye, character is the real you. This is the product of your natural temperament that is modified by your childhood education, training, principles, basic attitudes, beliefs, and other motivations. It is sometimes referred to as "The soul" of man, which is made up of the mind, emotions and will. Your character says who you are. When one covers up his character without dealing with it to effect a total change and begin to act in acceptable ways in order to belong, it only complicates the matter because the real person must burst out one day and beside the person will be living in deception. This is what Psychologist called Personality. Tim Lahaye, again, defined personality as outward expression of ourselves, which may or may not be the same as our character, depending on how genuine we are. According to him Personality is often, a pleasing façade for an unpleasant or weak character. It is the face we want to show others. Let me illustrate with this short story:

A scorpion, being a poor swimmer, asked a turtle to carry him on his back across a river. "Are you mad?" exclaimed the turtle. "You will sting me while I'm swimming and I'll drown."

My dear turtle, laughed the scorpion, If I sting you, you will sink and I will also go down with you. Now, where is the logic in that?

"You are right," cried the turtle. "Hop on!"

The scorpion climbed aboard and halfway across the rivers gave the turtle a mighty sting. As both of them sank to the bottom of river, the turtle said, Can I ask you a question? You said clearly that there would be no logic at all in your stinging me. Why then did you do if? This one has nothing to do at all with logic, the drowning scorpion replied very sadly . "It's just my character." (J. Maurus, 1987).

Even though, reason and logic says scorpion can't do that but he did it. Even though scorpion says he wouldn't do it and made up his mind not to do it, he did it because it (stinging) has become part of him. It is his character even though he tried to hide it still reveals itself. Work on your character and not personality. "Most people would rather work on their personality than their character and now right he is. Perhaps that is because the personality development brings more immediate rewards, is less demanding and, in most cases, involves little sacrifice on our part. personality development involves learning new conversational skills, style, or developing a speaking ability. The development of character is more profound, is considerably more difficult, and often involves making changes that are at least temporarily uncomfortable and often very demanding. The changing of habits is always a difficult procedure. The development of virtues also require time because it means we must discipline some of our appetites and passions. Keeping promises and being sensitive to the feelings and convictions of others are not things that most of us do naturally. We have to work at them. Development of character is the best sign of maturity." (Zig Ziglar, 1999)

Finally, when a thorough knowledge of self is acquired, it will help one to behold how far he is ready to give himself to God and will identify all those creatures that stands between him and God. Unless this is done, one may continue in pursuit of vain glory and justifying error. Therefore, go into prayer closet, shut your door to the outside world, and open up yourself to the Holy Spirit who sees you as you are so that He will renew you.

This I say to you and testify in the Lord, that you should walk no longer as the rest of the Gentiles do, in the futility of their mind, with their understanding clouded and separated from the life of the Almighty God, because of their stack ignorance, due to of the darkness in their heart; who, being past feeling, have completely given themselves to filthiness, to work all uncleanness with greediness. But you have not learned such from Christ if really you have heard Him and have been taught by Him, as the truth is in our Lord Jesus Christ: that you cast out, your past and former conduct, the old self, the corrupt flesh, which is very corrupt according to the deceitful lusts, and be totally renewed and be transformed in the spirit of your mind, and that you put on the new man which was formed according to God

Almighty, in true righteousness and holiness (Eph. 4: 17-24).

3. PRACTICAL DECISION

A sound appraisal of oneself when properly done will help one identify all those faults and bad habits that keep you away from God, but these have to be followed by a very practical decision to follow Christ in everyday life. It should be done with all seriousness no matter what harm it will cause to our personal and social life. Jesus says, "No one who puts his hand to the plow and looks back is fit for service in the kingdom of God." Much effort should be done to replace all those vices identified with virtues. "Bad habits are evil inclinations acquired through repeated bad acts. Unless we overcome these habits, they will gradually become our master." (My Daily Bread). Thomas a Kempis tells us that "Habit is overcome by habit" (My Imitation of Christ). By Continuous effort to acquire good habits we replace the bad one through the Grace of God.

A Practical decision to follow Christ involves upholding the will of God regardless of the pain or pleasure one derives from it. It is a life of total surrender to the will of God, both in riches and in poverty; both to in need and in luxury. That is repeating the same prayer Christ made to the Father, "All I have is yours" (John 17:10b) and working strongly to live it out. You are alone in this for the Grace of God will always be there to assist you. Rev. Fr. Anthony Paone says: "Just how sincere we are when we say that we love Christ, is seen in our daily effort for perfection. God will not judge us by our failures, but rather, by our efforts. He wants us to try, and to keep trying, to become the kind of person He wants us to be. Over confidence shows our selfishness. Only a humble, determined, and persevering effort can prove genuine love for Christ."

4.   A PROGRAMME OF LIFE

St. Benedict, one of the early fathers of the Church, bequeathed a precious spiritual treasurer to the Christian world-the Rule of St Benedict. A modest book which has sent countless of Saints to heaven and its great impacts both on the clergy and the laity are still felt even in the modern times and the result cannot be over emphasized even at the present times. When Benedict began to organize his monks at Subiaco and Monte Cassino, we were told that monks had no common life, they tried to outdo each other in austerities, and they wandered about from monastery to monastery as their fancy dictated, they recited as many as all the Psalms of David a day, added to too many other prayers and devotions. But in all these the monks never found holiness until St. Benedict formed a programme of life for them. St. Benedict fashioned a life centered around a common task-the chanting of the Opus Dei, or Divine Office - and dedicated to useful labor, both intellectual and physical, as well as to private prayer and reasonable forms of penance. This programme of life gave their resolution a form of permanency and was characterized by a certain degree of constancy and even regularity.

Beloved, your desire to live a life of prayer – a devote life cannot be easily actualized without a definite and orderly planned programme of life that will help you to be constantly and always in tune with God. St Paul says "Pray at all times in the Spirit, with all prayer and supplication." Adequate planning is necessary to achieve success in everything one does. So it is in prayer and even more. If you pray only when you are in need or feel like praying or on Sunday morning or fellowship days you will never build a prayer life. There fore you need to prayerfully develop a set programme that will serve as spiritual guide to you. Those in religious order are bound with a particular one acceptable to them, but under the guidance of the Holy Spirit you can develop your own program that will suit your vocation, profession and life style. Devotions are possible in all profession. What is needed is adequate planning and a programme that will be compatible with ones vocation. St Francis de Sales says that there is different kinds of devotion (prayer life) for the gentleman and the artisan; for the servant and the prince; for the wife, the maiden, and the widow; and still further, the practice of devotion must be adapted to capabilities, the engagements, and the duties of each individual."

Such a programme should bear a fixed time for your quiet time that suits you best, with adequate provision for other devotions. Make provision for fasting, if you can fast, bearing in mind that fasting must not only be from food. Bring in other pieties and corporal works of mercy as the Spirit leads you. Stick to this and struggle to observe it until it becomes part of you.

Don't just make it a habit but a way of life. Let every part of you yearn for it. Let it change your whole being. Then thousands of times in the day offer your soul to him, fix your inward eyes on his kindness, and hold out your hand to him as a child to his father. This kind of spirit union can be achieved by the use of aspiration and ejaculatory prayers as we described earlier. When properly done, this instead of beings a hindrance to one's duty helps it. All this should be done in a spirit of humility without any intention whatsoever to show off, otherwise pride will crop in to reduce the whole thing to nothing.

There are so many figures in the scripture who's established programme of life kept them constantly in tune with God. I will begin with Abraham, our father in faith. What do you understand from the texts below?

Abram took his tents and moved to live close the terebinth of Mamre, which is at Hebron. At this place, he built an altar to the Lord God. (Gen. 13: 18)

The LORD appeared to Abraham by the terebinth of Mamre, as he sat in the entrance of his tent, while the day was growing hot. (Gen. 18:1)

Early the morning Abraham went to the place where he had stood in the LORD's presence. (Gen. 19:27)

Abraham has a deep prayer relationship with God. Immediately he arrived at Canaan, the land God sent him to, the first thing he thought of was to build an alter to the Lord. This led him to locate a cool and quite spot, under an oak tree called terebinth of Mamre at Hebron. Abraham went there from time to time to encounter God. On waking up, very early in the morning, Abraham would go there to encounter God, at the heat of the day, he would return there to meet Him, at the cool of the day he would return there with evening sacrifice. This is the secret of Abraham's success and power. Abraham never took any important decision in life without going there to discuss it with God first. Today, we sing of Abraham's blessings, but how many of us will remember the last meeting we had with the Lord for a life changing encounter or remember discussing with the Lord before signing a contract or embarking on a serious business. Remember prayer unlocks every spiritual blessing; a man of prayer never fails. A University professor was asked why he wakes up as early as 4am to pray and he answered: "Prayer is the secret of my success and since I want to keep on succeeding, I will keep praying; take it away from me I am gone." Negligence of prayer is a sign of failure. Being today, set apart a place and a time of meeting with the Lord, and keep to it. Visit him again and again; from time to time withdraw into the internal recess of your heart and adore the God that loves you so much.

Another great figure of the Old Testament worthy of mention is David, listen to him.

I rise early and cry for help O God; I have put all my hope in your word O Lord my God. My eyes are always open throughout the watches of the night, that I may medicate on your word. (Ps. 119:14).

My soul waits eagerly for the Lord God more than night guard wait for the morning, more than night guard wait for the morning. (Ps. 130: 6).

In the morning, O Lord my God, you listen to my voice; early in the morning I make my requests before you O God and wait in full expectation. (Ps. 5:3).

As the deer yearn for streams of living water, so my soul thirsts for you, O Lord my God. My soul yearns for

God, for the living God. When can I go and be with my God? (Ps.42:1-2).

All the people that made great impact in the Scriptures were people of prayer. Reading through the verses above, one will understand that prayer was not just David's weapon of warfare but part of him. His whole body yearns for it. It is the secret of his power. In his early life. David tended his father's flocks, "thereby being trained for his subsequent career, for he had ample scope for quiet and prayerful meditations such as Moses had in his 40 years retirement in Midian before his call to public life, and as Paul had in the Arabian sojourn (Gal. 1:17) before his worldwide ministry. Those who are to be great public men often need first to be great in the secret meeting with God. David was indeed a man after God's heart. His intimate acquaintance with the beauties of nature, like water, fields, hills, the forest, and the sun, moon, and glorious heavens above, gives coloring to many of his psalms (Ps. 29; Ps. 8; Ps. 19, ect.)." (Fausset's Bible Dictionary). There are so many examples of great warriors in the Scripture but time and space wouldn't allow me to enumerate them. The few I have done is to spur you to get started. Begin it right now, the time is ripe. I will now discuss other things you need to watch out as you progress in your quiet time.

SPIRITUAL CONSOLATION

Spiritual consolation is spiritual delight and comfort granted by God to souls during meditation or quiet time. It is entirely a gift from God. It is not out of any merit of the soul. It is a free gift from God. It is most times given to spur the soul to a greater height. It may come in the form of revelations from God, prophesy, internal joy and happiness, holy dreams, strong feeling of Divine presence, ecstasy and other spiritual manifestation. Fr. Anthony Paone S.J in My Daily Bread said "Spiritual consolation is only a temporary gift to encourage one who is earnestly trying to serve Me. This gift is not at the command of any man, and it will not be given to anyone who seeks it for itself. Such a person is too much like the man who seeks his entire happiness in the pleasures, satisfactions, and honors of this world. A frank and intelligent remembrance of your unworthiness will help you perform your prayers and good works without expecting spiritual consolations in return." Beloved as you progress in this spiritual journey you may experience at one time or the other an inward consolation and holy inspiration, like Jacob in Gen. 32, let it help you ascend higher but don't use it to judge your progress. It is given by God to whom he will at the time he wills. It entirely depends on him and not on you. Beware, where you seek this indiscriminately, Satan may hijack it and begin to tell you what you want to hear or begin to show what you want to see, beware. Just depend on God, and be an instrument in His hand, He will use you as He wishes and lead you where He wants you to go. St. Francis de Sales write: if it pleases the Almighty God to speak with us, to hold dialogue with us by His most holy inspirations and inward consolations, it is doubtless a great honor and unspeakable delight; but if He vouchsafes not so to favour, neither speaking, nor even appearing to perceive us, as though we were in His presence; therefore, we must not leave our prayers: on the contrary, we must remain devoutly and meekly before His sovereign goodness, and then He will assuredly accept our patience, and observe our assiduity and perseverance, so that when we again come before him, He will look favorably on us, and reward us with His consolations, bidding us taste the sweetness of devout prayer."

SPIRITUAL ARIDITY

Having talked about spiritual consolation, now I am going tell you about what most writers called Spiritual Aridity, or dryness. It can also be called Desert Experience. Aridity came from the word "arid." It is a land that is so dry that only very few plants can grow in it. Arid is also used to describe a situation that is dull that is completely lacking in interest or excitement. Aridity, therefore, means dryness, barrenness, infertility and so on. So, Spiritual Aridity is a state of spiritual dryness experienced by a soul on its journey to perfection. As you advance in your prayer life you may notice that at times or at a particular stage, that the normal delight and inward consolations that do characterize your prayer may no longer come and your prayer will seems so dry. The revelations, prophesy and the excitements that you usually experience may no longer come. Don't be discouraged if you experience such a situation, it does not mean that God is far off from you or that he doesn't listen to you any longer. He is even closer to you at this time than ever, the Saints teaches that at this times God is drawing you out of yourself to himself. So that you will learn to pray for the love of God, you worship God because he is God and not because of the consolation and things you receive from him. This is a time of solid food and not milk. A time Jesus wants you to go beyond the gifts he gives to behold him and possess him the giver of the gift. (See john 6) So that you can say with Paul, I no longer live but Christ lives in me.

My life has been crucified with Christ Jesus and it is no longer I who live, but Christ Jesus lives in me. This very life in the body, I live with full faith in the Son of God, who loved me so much and gave himself for me. (Gal. 2:20).

So, let not such dryness discourage you. Instead of discouraging you, let it even make you to fire on. Knowing that He is even closer than ever, for if you persist, you shall be plunged into Him and begin to savour the glorious riches in Christ.

CHAPTER FIVE

PEACE AMIDST TURMOIL

A doctor who had many patients that were in the large income brackets made a study of why they worried so much. Here is what he found. 40% of their worries were about things that never happened 30% were about matters entirely beyond their control.

12% were related to the physical ills, which were caused or increased by their emotional attitudes. 10% were about friends or relatives who were quite able to look after themselves.

Only 8% were about matters that really needed their attention –but worry even in these cases was not remedy to apply.

Peace is the greatest gift of God to Mankind. Perhaps, that is why Jesus is called the Prince of Peace. (Is. 9:5). The glorious choir of the Angels at the birth of Christ echoed Peace: Glory to God in the highest, and on earth peace to men on whom his favour rest. And to confirm this, our Saviour himself breathed this peace upon the Apostle after the resurrection saying: Peace be with you! (John 20:19)

In talking of peace here, I do not mean just freedom from war or violence or am I just talking of freedom from conflict or disagreement among people or groups of people, but that state of mental calmness and serenity, devoid of all anxiety; that interior quietness and tranquility; that inner contentment that characterizes the soul that embodies the Holy Spirit. Peace is not a function of the environment but of the mind. A peaceful sow and cultivate an atmosphere of peace wherever he goes, but you need one chaotic mind to disrupt and distort a peaceful atmosphere. Make the mind to be in peace and it will breathe peace to everything and everyone around it but distort it and it will cause untold harm both to the person concerned, his neighbours and the environment at large. A man of peace is a priceless worth.

I included this chapter to help you experience the peace of soul, without which it will be very difficult to observe your quiet time or practice mind or mental prayer. If the outside world is noisy, hustling, troubled and confused that we cannot find solace in it, then we must have a way of retiring back into our soul and to enjoy real tranquility and peace. This is the only thing that will make our prayer possible and enable us dwell deep in His presence. The Saints know this and that is the secret of their prayer life. They know that God dwells in their heart. Therefore, from time to time they retire back to it to take refuge from the daily anxieties. In order to pray, therefore, we need to develop or acquire a serene and composed heart that knows no agitation but peace in the midst of troubles, anxieties and fears. Christ says:

Remember, I have told you all these things, so that you may have peace in me. In this world you will have trouble. But take heart! I have overcome the world. (John16:33)

Jesus is not saying that troubles wouldn't be there. Surely problem will come, difficulties and vicissitudes of life will be there, there will be distractions but in the midst of all these, Jesus says "Peace!" Take heart! Let nothing trouble you for I have overcome the world. The victory of Jesus is our victory- this is the joy and peace of the elect. The world does not know it neither can it give such peace. It is not found in money or wealth. Human security cannot provide it. Drugs or entertainment cannot give it. It only comes from the Prince of Peace- Our Lord Jesus Christ. He is ever assuring us "Peace I leave with you; my peace I give you. I do not give to you as the would gives. Do not let hearts be troubled and do not be afraid." But how does one really experience this peace of soul?

EYES ON JESUS AND NOT ON PROBLEM

A song writer once wrote "God is bigger than every mountain, I can or cannot see." When you become engrossed or overwhelmed by the enormity of your problem, it blinds you from seeing the solution but when we keep your eyes on the solution, it lifts us above human difficulties and problems. This is always true. In chapter 14 of St. Matthew Gospel, at the instance of Jesus, Peter began to walk on water. As long as he kept his eyes on Jesus, he continued to walk on the water, but he began to sink as soon his eyes caught the turbulent sea and he was overwhelmed. Don't allow problems to distract you, no matter how big it is, keep your eyes on Jesus. A young boy that felt so relaxed in the midst of a troubled boat, to greatest chagrin of all other passengers on board was questioned "Boy, don't you know that this boat is about to capsize, are you not touched?" And his answer was short and simple "My father is the Captain; I know he is in control." Beloved I tell you something Jesus is in control – relax. Let me also share my own experience with you to buttress this. I was so much disturbed and worried, laying in a hospital bed at a certain time. This is not only because of the high fever I was diagnosed of and the increased heart beat and pains that accompanied it but the thought of what would be my fate also disturbed my spirit. I couldn't sleep or even say any serious prayer; I was highly disturbed. It was in this confused state that I heard a still voice that said to me "don't worry, I am in control" The voice was so strong that it cleared all my fears and anxieties. With this confidence that the Lord is in control I muttered prayers, committed myself and the situation into God's hands and slept off. Four hours later, I woke up fully healed. It baffled the doctor and the nurses who had collected all my personal data, thinking that I wouldn't survive. Instead of looking at how big, difficult and complicated your situation is, look at the supremacy and the power of Jesus to change situations.

This will keep your eyes on him and the more you look at him the more your problem fizzle away. I conclude this section with a word of wisdom from Mildred Allen Jeffery:

Last night I started counting sheep

    When I had gone to bed,

For I had worries large and small

Which drove sleep from my head.

The Sheep had many little lambs,

    And these I counted too;

Thus through the flock I went until

The Shepherd came in view.

And then I thought, "Why spend my time

In simple counting sheep

When I can walk with Him and pray

For folks who cannot sleep?"

I walked with him a while and then

He smiled and said to me,

"look back, where are your worries now?"

but not one could I see!

GOD HAS A PLAN FOR YOUR LIFE

A professor of Mathematics was once questioned on the possible solution to African unemployment problem and his answer was short and simple – "Planning." He said that in America before a graduate is produced that there is always a place for him in the Industries. That America never produces a graduate without building an industry where he is going to apply his knowledge and skills. So, the more they build universities, the more they build industries that will absorb the graduate so that they will not waste away.

If human beings can plan like this, how much more God who is a master planner. God didn't just create you for nothing. No, there is a plan for your life, even before you were created. You were not just thrown into the earth aimlessly to determine your fate. No, there is a purpose for your life. And the truth is that nothing can change this God's purpose for your life unless you bluntly reject it; Satan cannot change it; enemies cannot change it; even your sin can only delay it but cannot change it as long as you remain focused. Satan tormented Job so much that he lost everything he had including his health, but he was not able to change God's plan for him because at the appointed time Job began to smile again. The Bible says that the Lord God made him very prosperous again and gave him double his former possession.

The sons of Jacob tried all they could to deal with Joseph and prevent his dream of being a king among them from coming through. They beat him up; threw him into a pit; sold him as slave to Egypt and he was thrown into prison but still at God's appointed time, God's purpose for his life still came to pass.

And Pharaoh told Joseph: I do hereby place you totally in charge of this Land, Egypt. So, pharaoh took his ring from his finger and put it gentle on Joseph's finger. He had him dressed in robes of fine and costly linen and put a gold chain on his neck. He made ride in a chariot as his next-in-command, and men were shouting before him, "make a way!" In this way, he placed him in totally charge of all the land of Egypt. And Pharaoh told Joseph: I'm Pharaoh, but without your command no one will raise hand or foot in all the land of Egypt. (Gen. 41:41-44)

These brothers of his tracked him down to Egypt to worship him. Israelite sinned against the Lord and received one punishment after another to the point that they spent forty years in a journey of forty days but this did not stop God's plan for their life because as many of them that were able to stand up from their iniquity and look unto God, still inherited that promise. You are created for a purpose and nothing can change that God's purpose for your life as long as you remain focused in him who alone is the reason for your existence. Let this thought keep your heart in peace. All you have to do is to begin to live a life of inheritance, letting nothing disturb your Spirit. The Bible says: Do not let your hearts be troubled. Trust in me and also trust in God (John 14:1a)

Do not be worried about anything at all, but in everything, through prayer and petition, with total thanksgiving, present your all requests to God Almighty. And the peace of the Lord our God, which surpasses all understanding, will keep your heart and your minds in Jesus Christ. (Philippians 4:6-7)

The Scripture is very emphatic on this "do not let your heart be troubled", just trust in the saving power of God, knowing that at the appointed time he will lift you up. When your time comes, Satan can't stop it; enemies can't prevent; situations will bow for you because heaven is making a move, which no force can change. Just keep your heart in peace and wait for the appointed time for the plan of God must come to fulfillment. The Bible says if it delays wait for it.

I shall climb my watch tower and wait, listening to know what he will say to me, the answer he will give to my request. Then, the Lord God answered me and said;

write this vision down clearly, inscribe it on tablets can easily be   read. For this vision has its appointed time, it hastens towards its end and it will not delay; if it takes some time, wait for it, for surely it shall come. (Hab. 2:1 -3)

Dear, you are so precious a creature that God will never fail to accomplish the purpose of your creation. Relax, it is God's Project. He will perfect what he started.

WHERE THERE IS ORDER, THERE MY PEACE WILL DEWEL

My Child, as I have already told you, where there is order there will you find My peace. My peace does not leave you until some disorder has entered into your soul. This disorder may be in your thinking or in your will (My Daily Bread)

Order is an organized state, with elements arranged properly, neatly, harmoniously. Zig Ziglar once asked a beautiful question: can you remember a day you did not have some "problems", irritation, disappointment, defeat, or setback of some kind? According to him, the big issue is not the problems; they are part of life. The issue is how to handle the problem. On another occasion, he wrote We live in a fast-moving world, and despite all the timesaving, labour saving approaches and devices available to us today, despite all the technology for streamlining, it seems that our wishes and desires require more additional time than the new technology and planning can provide. What this really means is we need to prioritize what is important to 'keep the main thing the main thing.

Adequate planning of our day and everything we do is very necessary for a peaceful living. Some of the things that distract you especially during your quiet time, most of the time, include unfinished duties and duties unattended to. Plan your day well and do not let things come in to disrupt the order of priority. I asked a Christian Brother for the time of his Morning Prayer and he told me "whenever I wake up" – Serious! And I asked again, what of your evening prayer and another interesting answer came immediately; "when I'm about to go bed." Such a carefree, lazy and unplanned life can never make a prayer warrior. Yes, because at that time of the night he is sure to battle sleep and hurtful memories because the body is weak and late in the morning pressure and anxieties may set in that most of the time, he may hardly pray before leaving the house. Let everything has its rightful place in your life. Attend to your duties trusting in God and not working as if to say everything depends on you. The scripture says: in vain do you wake up so early, and put off going to bed, sweating to make a living, since it is he who provides for his beloved as they sleep. (Ps. 127;2 NJB) Rest when you are to do so. Don't spend a longer time than necessary watching television, surfing the web, or in amusement parks. Try to avoid idle discussion. Spend more time with Lord because the more you come closer to him the more you experience interior peace and the more your happiness will be.

Your planning, some time, may not prevent problems and setbacks of life from coming when it will come, but decide on one thing, not to allow those problems direct you, dictate your action or decide on how you live your life, but see them as opportunities for greater glory. They can be handled by simply renewing your mind and seeing them as opportunities to grow and mature. Instead of allowing them to distract us in prayer, we should see it as wounds Jesus will heal and allow Him to touch us with his healing power. Don't ever allow any problem to overwhelm you no matter how big it is, even when you can't see immediate solution, always look at heaven and see the source of your existence – He is bigger than any human problem. Your life depends on Him and not even in your hand. Dwell in him and forget all your worries, He is aware of them all.

ACCEPT THE WILL OF GOD FOR YOUR LIFE

There is only one way to true and lasting peace. That way is God's will. The man who lacks interior peace either wants what God does not want him to have, or refuses to take what God wants him to take. One who does his best to embrace God's holy will, will receive Christ's peace. What about me? Am I trying to embrace God's holy will in all that happens to me each day? I must see God directing, supporting, and permitting whatever occurs, be it good or evil. In allowing evil to happen, God has reasons far beyond my understanding. My highest wisdom lies in embracing the evils which I am not able to remedy, accepting them because God permitted them to happened to me. When I have succeeded in wanting only what God wants me to have, I shall know the wonderful peace of Christ. (My Daily Bread).

"Oh God, where are you?" "Why me?" 'What kind of life is this?" These and many other questions arise when one finds himself in a terrible situation or long-term suffering or in a condition that seems unfavourable to him but in all these situations, it is only one who readily accepts the will of God that will experience interior peace. It is true you may not understand why God allowed a particular situation in your life or why God made you the way you are, but relax because there is a purpose for your life and our God is a master planner he cannot fail. Just wait on him. You are just like clay in the hands of God who is the potter. He is moulding and remoulding you in order to bring out the best in you. The way he puts you is the way you will shine best. Surrender to God and his plan for your life will come true. The Book of Jeremiah speaks on this:

This is the word of the Lord that came to Jeremiah from heaven: Go down to the potter's house, and there I will give you my message. So, I went to the potter's house, and I saw him working at the wheel. But the pot he was shaping from the clay was marred in his; so, the potter formed it into another pot, shaping it as seemed best to him. Then God spoke to me: can I not do with you the way this potter does, oh house of Israel? Like ordinary clay in the hands of this potter, so you are in my hand, O house of Israel. (Jeremiah 18:1-6)

The Lord knows how best to bring you to the finishing points; how best to make you shine; how best to bring you to glory. Jesus prayed for the Father's will and not his will. Heavenly Father, if it is your will, may this cup be taken away from me. Not my will, but your will oh Lord. (Mat. 26:39).

It is the will of the father that he will undergo the pains of Calvary because that is the only way he can enter his Glory. The situation you are in is not meant to "kill" you but that through it you will enter your Glory.

For our light and momentary troubles are achieving for us an eternal glory that far out weights them all. As we place our eyes not on what is visible, but on what is invisible. For what is visible is temporary, but what is invisible will last forever. (2 Cor. 4:17-18).

For as you greatly rejoice that though you may suffer grief in all types of trails for a little while now. These came so that your precious faith—that worth more than gold, which fades though refined by fire—may prove to be very genuine and will result in praise, honor, and glory when Christ Jesus is revealed. (1 Peter 1:6-7).

May the Almighty God, who chose us for His everlasting glory in Christ Jesus, after you have suffered a little while, perfect, strengthen, settle and establish you. To Him alone be all the glory and the dominion both now and forever Amen. (1 Peter 5:10-1).

Don't allow your condition or your situation to depress you. Peace of soul lies in accepting those things you cannot change and making the best out of it. I tell you the story of Juliana (I changed the name) who is happily married to a young, handsome and wealthy man. Juliana studied Pharmacy and graduated with honours. As at the time of writing, she already had two sons for her husband. Juliana has bad legs and can't walk because of Polio infection that she suffered at her early years. She uses a wheelchair. This is Juliana's condition, but she didn't allow this her condition to hinder her an inch. The condition didn't prevent her from getting married to her husband and reaching the height of her career. Juliana does every work of a housewife and even works in a drug manufacturing company to support the family. Her condition did not hinder her. She is a happy woman.

Accepting your condition doesn't mean accepting failure but recognizing the love of God over you even in that your condition and believing God that He has a reason for allowing you pass through it. This will keep your heart in peace and wake you up to do exploit even in the face of that condition. Worries blinds our mind eyes from seeing solutions to our problem but peace drives away every darkness, fear, and ushers in Christ who is the way even where there is no way. To those who believe in God, there is hope even in the most hopeless condition. Their hope is that because Christ lives, they will live no matter what the condition is. So instead of lamenting your situation, stand up and make the best use of it and you will see the love of God taking you through. While you are crying, lamenting and worrying, all you will see are darkness and failures, but the moment you stand up and wipe away your tears, you begin to see the light of salvation. The problem will fizzle away and you will begin to live.

TRUE AND LASTING PEACE IN GOD ALONE

Finally, true and lasting peace lies only in God. It is only found in doing the will of God. There can be no true peace outside God. St Augustine says "God you created us only for yourself and our heart will not rest until it rests in you." When you seek for this peace in the things created, no matter the satisfaction you get from those things it cannot give true peace because they are only but reflections of the creator who alone is the true source of happiness and lasting peace. Archbishop Fulton Sheen says: your unhappiness is not due to your want of fortune or high position or fame or sufficient vitamins. It is due not to a want of something outside of you, but to a want of something inside of you. You were made for perfect happiness. No wonder nothing except God disappoints you. These words are further strengthened by the following verses from My Daily Bread by Fr. Anthony Paone, SJ:

My child, when you have risen so high in virtue that you seek comfort and satisfaction from Me before all earthly remedies, I shall bestow on you the grace of knowing Me intimately and of enjoying My friendship as never before. Your interior peace will no longer be disturbed by daily events. No more will you be attached to what you have, nor complain about what you lack. You will place yourself entire in My hands. I shall be your main interest, and nothing will ever again take My place in your life.

I am the fountain of true peace and lasting joy. Keep close to Me in your daily life. The man whose main interest are on earth, does not know the meaning of true peace. His joys are temporary and rapidly passing. No person or thing on earth can fully satisfy the thirst within your soul. You were made for Me, and I alone can bring you the perfect, all-satisfying happiness which you seek.

This supernatural friendship requires that you give your heart entirely to Me. This simply means that you will give due attention to every person and every duty in your daily life, without giving them any more attention and time than they deserve. Your main desire must be to give Me all the attention and time possible each day.

If you make reservations in your self-surrender, if in anything you seek your own desires rather than My will, you will be hindering Me from giving you the special graces which I want to bestow on you. Your union with Me will be imperfect and you will not be ready for My higher gifts. Offer me the actions of your day. Repeat your offering at different times, and renew your intention to shut out all worldly self-seeking. In due time, you have proved yourself, you will receive My most wonderful graces. (My Daily Bread)

INTERIOR PEACE AND QUIET TIME

A distressed soul cannot genuinely observe quiet time. Quiet time is only possible for a peaceful heart. That is why I have taken time to present the above to you so that your heart may experience the only true and lasting peace that can keep you in God's presence. Let the above words help keep your heart in peace. Don't allow anything to steal it from you. Struggle hard to maintain it until you are completely absorbed in Christ, the Prince of Peace.

CHAPTER SIX

ALL THINGS ARE YOURS

So then, no more boasting about men! All things are yours, whether it is Paul or Cephas or Apollos or life or death or the world or the present or the future – all are yours, and you are of Christ Jesus, and Christ Jesus is of God. (1 Cor. 3:21-22).

Do you know that you are wonderfully made? You were not just created like every other creature. You were specially made – the summit of all creation. You are glorious because you were made in the image and likeness of the glorious God. The Bible says: Let us make man in our own image and likeness and let them rule all over the fishes of the sea and all the birds of the air, over all livestock, over all the whole earth, and over all the creatures that live on the ground. (Gen. 1:26-27).

After your wonderful creation. God didn't just end there he handed everything to you - the whole earth and made you the lord of them all – an exalted position and further ordained and blessed you to increase and multiply:

The Almighty God blessed man and commanded him to be fruitful and increase and fill the whole earth and subdue it. He commanded him to rule over the all fish of the sea and all the birds of the air and over every creature that lives on the ground. The Almighty God said: I give you every plant that is bearing seed on the face of the earth and every tree that bears fruit. They will be all yours for food. And to all the animals of the earth and all the birds that live in the air and all the creatures that live the ground—everything that has the breath – I give you every green plant for your food. And so, it was. (Gen. 1:28-30).

My dear this is your position as child of God. You are placed in this position by God himself. God first of all created and filled the earth with good things and after then created you to govern all of them. This is the divine ordination for your life. God wonderfully made you and provided everything for you in order that you might rejoice and be happy.

Rejoice in the Lord always. I shall say it again: rejoice! (Phil. 4:4).

This is the purpose and plan of God for you. Therefore, everything that stands against this Divine ordination for your life is not from God because God cannot change his ways. The Bible says: The Almighty God is not like a man, that he should tell lie, nor a son of man, that he should change his mind. Does he speak and then not act? Does he promise and not fulfill? (Num. 23:19). All you only need to do is rise up and behold what is yours. This is not a question of crying or complaining or fighting for it. No – it is your right. You have the legal right of ownership of all things – the earth and its fullness. It is given to you by God himself. All you need to do is to rise up and take what is already yours. It is only a prince who is ignorant of his position as a prince and what his father kept in stock for him that eats from the dust.

THE REDEMPTIVE WORK OF CHRIST

The gate of heaven was closed against man when Adam and Eve sinned. (Gen. 3:23-24). Man was then sent out to suffer and to cultivate the soil. Evil from this moment entered the world. The situations and creatures man was supposed to command and control began to kill him. Who will deliver man from this situation? No one, not even the patriarchs can help. John says:

I noticed that the one who sits on the throne was holding a scroll that was written on the front and back and it was sealed with a total of seven seals. Then I saw a powerful angel who called with a loud voice, who is worthy to open the scroll and break its seal? But no one was able to open the scroll and read it both in heaven or on the earth or under the earth, I bitterly wept because there was no one to open the scroll and also read it. (Rev. 5:1-4).

Since man can't help himself out of the situation, Jesus our Lord, the only begotten son of God came down on earth, took our nature and became man in order to lead us out of the dungeon back to glory. John tells us:

And one of the elders told me; Weep not! See, the Lion from the tribe of Judah, the Root of Jesse, has conquered. He has the power to open the scroll with all of its seven seals. And I saw a Lamb, appearing as if it was slain, standing at the center of the throne, surrounded by the elders and the four living creatures. He had seven eyes with seven horns eyes, which are the seven spirits of the Almighty God sent out into the whole of the earth. He stood up and took the scroll from the right hand of him who was sitting on the throne. (Rev. 5:5-7).

Christ came to restore us back to our glory. The glory man lost at the Garden of Eden because of Adam was fully restored back on the cross of Calvary through the death of Christ. The revelation of John continues:

Then they started singing a new song: you are all worthy to take this scroll and open its seals. This is because you were slain, and by your blood, you delivered men to Almighty God from every race and language and nation and people. (Rev. 5:9).

Therefore, by the reason of Jesus death upon the cross of Calvary, we were set free from all our iniquities, restored to the heavenly blessings and glory. We are now heirs of the kingdom and no longer slaves. Once again, we have taken back our first position as the glory of all creation to control and command situations. The force of evils, problems, and difficulties has no control over us again because Christ has nailed it to the cross. What we lost because of the disobedience of Adam we now gained fully in Christ.

And even when you were dead (in) transgressions and the uncircumcision of your flesh, he brought you to life along with him, having forgiving us all out transgressions; obliterating the bondage against us, with its lawful claims, which was against us, he also removed it completely from our midst, nailing it on the cross; despoiling the powers and principalities, he made a completely public spectacle of them, leading them away in a victory parade. (Col. 2:13-15).

Christ, first of all, wiped our iniquities and canceled every record of our sin and then dealt with everything that held us captive – setting us free from every bondage, curse, debt and oppression due to our sin and devil so that in him we might be reconciled to God. (cc Romans 5:10). After having made us children and co-heirs of the kingdom, he then filled us with every blessing in the heavenly places so that in him we might be complete and lacking nothing.

The Holy Spirit itself bears witness with our own spirit that we are sons and daughters of God, and if children, then heirs, heirs of God and joint-heirs with Christ Jesus, if only we endure and suffer with him in order that we may also be glorified with him. (Romans 8:16-17).

Thanks be to Almighty God, our heavenly father, and father of our saviour Jesus Christ, who has endowed us with all spiritual blessing in the heavenly realms in Christ Jesus. (Eph. 1:3).

This is what Christ did for you. It is not out of any merit of yours. It is by the Grace of God and Grace means an unmerited favour – A free gift from God. The Bible says: God, our heavenly father, shows his own love for us in this: while we were still sinners, Christ Jesus died for us. (Rom. 5:8). You are qualified for this heavenly blessing and glorious inheritance by Christ death. The Scripture says: giving thanks to God the Father, who has made you qualified to share in the inheritance of the saints of God in the kingdom of light and glory. Because he has delivered us from the kingdom of darkness and brought us into the kingdom of his dear Son, our Lord Jesus Christ. (Col. 1:12).

Beloved, you know what, Christ has done everything for you. The healing you are asking for has been granted by him (1 Pet. 2:24), the favour and all the Graces you need in life has also been granted (2 Pet. 1:3). All you need is to plunge yourself into Christ to take your share in this inheritance of the saints. In Christ, the transgressions of Adam were wiped and we were recreated to enjoy the Blessings of the ages. For we are God's masterpiece. He has made us a new in Christ Jesus, his dear son so that we can do the good things he planned for us before the ages began. (Eph. 2:10).

COME INTO THE KINGDOM

The prodigal son in Luke Chapter 15 languished and wasted away in suffering and was eating from crumbs until he realized that he was a prince; that he is not meant to eat from the crumbs or rot away in wretchedness but to reign as a prince. Listen to him:

And he longed to eat his fill of the pods on which swine fed, but nobody gave him any. When he came back to his senses, he said to himself, How many of my father's servants have food to spare, and here I am dying of starvation! I will stand up and go back to my father and I will tell him that I have sinned against him and against heaven. (Luke 15:16-18,

Once he realized himself that he was meant for the kingdom and not for pens, he stepped out and took what is his and his glory was restored.

The Genesis account stated the original state of man: his glorious and exalted position and kingdom. This is the state man was meant to be and was before the snare of the Devil eroded him of his position and his kingdom:

The Lord God sent man out the Garden of Eden to till the soil from which he had been taken. After he sent him out, he placed cherubim and a flaming sword flashing back and forth on the east side of the Garden of Eden to guard the way to the tree of life. (Gen. 3:23-24).

Man lost the kingdom and just like the prodigal son, he began to beg for crumbs instead of enjoying the kingdom banquet. Instead of complaining, crying, begging for crumbs find out first whether you have gone out of the kingdom where all blessings abound, if you have, get back and enjoy what is yours that has been ordained for you from the beginning. Can't you hear the Spirit say – "All things are yours!" Arise from your dungeon and take your position in the kingdom. A position Christ purchased for you with his blood. Therefore, by the reason of his blood you are a heir to his kingdom. Don't just settle for crumbs like the Canaanite woman. (Matt. 15:22-27) because you are a true child of Abraham in Jesus Christ. The only thing is for you to behold what has been done for you, open your arms and embrace it. Immediately the prodigal son realized himself, he got up and moved back to take back his position as prince. Jesus has opened for you a door which no man can close – a door to the kingdom, arise go in and you will enjoy the good things of the land. If you don't get back to the kingdom, you will only be picking crumbs because the kingdom food cannot be served in Egypt.

WE RECEIVE BY FAITH

Do you want to enjoy spiritual and glorious blessings in Christ? If your answer is yes, then you must be a man of faith. Do you want to take back your position and begin to command and control situation – the original position God gave man? Then you must be a man of faith, for faith unlocks every spiritual blessing and make physical that which already exists in the spiritual. The work has already been done; it is only left for the righteous to take if by faith (See. Hab. 2:4, Heb. 10:38). It is like a son that his father kept money for him in the bank but requires that he meets certain standards before colleting it. The money is already his but he has to accept it and make a move to pick it. By faith we believed in God and the power of His provision and He can do all things (See Job 42:2). Faith is a total conviction and blind trust in God, that even though we can't see Him physically, that He exists and that we are part of His glorious kingdom. By blind trust I don't mean acting in ignorance or without knowledge or wisdom but having full confidence in the greatness and omnipotence of God that he never fails no matter what the condition is. It is coming to grasp the eternal truth that even in the most hopeless condition that there is always a hope for those who trust in God. This is believing that God is able to cause a change no matter how deteriorated the situation may be. Having full confidence and trust in God, getting absorbed by it and allowing it to take the whole of you that when it comes to the things of God you are dead sure without shivering or staggering. Here is this story: A blind man walked into the school one day and was questioned by the school head: why are you putting on black shirt? And the blind man answered: I am putting on white shirt and not black. The school head knowing that the man is blind tries to convince him that the shirt is black and not white but the blind argued strongly: "it is not black; it is white for I know Johnny (his assistant) can't cloth me with any other shirt to school except white. I know he cannot fail. I have confidence that I am putting on white. My whole spirit tells me so and I believe it; every other testimony is false. After saying this he touched the shirt and said you are white; be white.

This is what I mean by blind trust and deep conviction. It rejects every other report even when reasons support such report. Jesus maintained that Lazarus was sleeping even when he was rotting away in the grave because he knew that even death is not an impossible case before God. (See John 11). There is a possibility that his boy Johnny made mistake or deliberately clothed him with black shirt. Yes, at least simple reason could have suggested that but he refused to believe it. Listen don't just die because doctor said that the illness is incurable. No, don't accept it, just stand up and live. The bible sums it up: Let the weak say, "I am strong.' "(Joel 3:10) and Strengthen your weak knees and feeble arm! Make smooth the way for your feet, so that what is cripple may not be disabled, but be healed. (Heb. 12:12).

DEVELOPING A MIRACLE WORKING FAITH

You may have received teaching again and again about the existence and omnipotence of God, may have confessed all these while that "you believe" but still within your heart, you know that you don't believe it. Your action tends to contradict your confession. What you act out in actual sense contradicts your claims. This is because faith is both an attitude of the spirit, which we freely exercise, and the gift of God. You have been saved by grace through faith, and that not by yourselves; it is the gift of God the Father (Eph. 2:8). In so many other portions of the scripture, we are exhorted to believe, trust or have faith. (Jn. 14:1, Acts

16:31). Faith goes beyond human mind and reasoning; it is a stance of the spirit. Therefore, to develop a working faith, one has to make effort, consistent effort to live out what he professes without hesitating while depending entirely on God who alone can reward your effort by giving you the gift of faith. Sinclair B. Ferguson et al, in New Dictionary of Theology, puts like this:

Both the Scripture and the Church tradition appear to say that faith is mysteriously both a divine gift and an uncoerced human activity.

Faith shouldn't end with believing only, you should act it out. St. James said;

Of what benefit is it, brother, if a man claims he has faith but no deeds? will that kind of faith save him? (James 2:14).

What makes your faith alive is when you act it out. Otherwise, it is dead. You can claim God's healing and miracle, but don't just end in claiming begin to live it out. Work it out. Even though you are still feeling pains in your body, begin to confess and act out the healing of Jesus, believing that it is already yours and it shall be yours. In one of my ministrations I led a lady suffering from a seasonal mental disorder to confess that she is healed and begin to act it out even though she still feels signs of the illness and the healing came. It was so dramatic. I was marveled also. Alleluia. The scripture says: I tell you, therefore, whatever you ask the Father in prayer, believe in your heart that you have already received it, and it shall be yours. (Mark 11:24). And St. James sums it up: Faith by itself, in like manner, if it is not followed with action is dead. (James 2:17).

The letter to the Hebrews chapter 11 verse 1 defined Faith as "the realization of what is hoped for and evidence of things not seen." The New Jerusalem Bible version puts it thus "only faith can guarantee the blessings that we hope for, or prove the existence of realities that are unseen." Faith substantiates God's promises, the fulfillment of which we hope, it makes them present realities. It is the evidence of things not seen.

Joseph Maurus told a story of a boy who was tightly gripping the cord as his kite soared way out of sight. A passer-by asked:

"What are you doing, boy?"

"Flying my kite," answered the lad.

"I cannot see any kite," objected the man

"Well, it is up there, way up there," said the boy with certainty.

"But how do you know it's up there?" the man went ahead

I can feel it's tug, Sir. That's how I know."

Christ has done everything for you. That is why he says "All things are yours." He blessed you with all the heavenly blessings and made you a heir to the kingdom. You can do all things because He strengths you. (See Phil. 4:19). The Bible says:

By his great power, he has endowed us with all the things we need for life and godliness, by the knowledge of him who called us by his own power and glory. (2 Pet. 1:3).

He has done all things well (mark 7:37). Everything is completed. It is only left for you to receive it by faith. Faith makes the promises and blessing of God realities in our life. The Bible says:

Now know this that the just shall live by faith; But if anyone goes back, my soul will find no pleasure in him. (Heb. 10:38)

Faith is a belief in, devotion to, or trust in somebody or something, especially without logical proof. Logic is a principle of valid reasoning and inference. It is based on sensible, rational thought and argument rather than ideas that are influenced by emotion or whim. Logic tries to prove everything scientifically, drawing conclusions based on facts, findings and results. Christianity is a matter of faith and not of logic. It is your faith in God that tells you that there is God. You have not seen him yet you believe that he exists and that he is the creator of the whole universe. Even though scientifically no one has proved this, yet our faith tells us that He Exists. Some even though they claim to believe in God find it difficult to believe in miracles because they approach it with logic and sort explanation in human reasoning. This may be because of their level of education. Unless one drops the wisdom of the world, he will never appreciate the healing power of God. Unless one become as flexible as a child and develop a childlike trust in God, he will find it difficult to appreciate the healing power of God.

I present to you again this story told by Tony de Mello of an interaction between a Guru (Spiritual Master) and an Atheist. I paraphrased it this time. An Atheist went to a Guru and asked "Do you believe in God? The Guru answered "Yes". "Can you proof to me that there is God" the Atheist retorted. The Guru answered with even more confidence "Yes" but before he could utter any other word the Atheist fired a third question: "Why are you so sure that you can convince me that there is God." And the Guru answered him in a manner and way that changed his life forever; he said "it is because even now I can see him more than I see you".

When you are puffed up with wisdom of the world it will erode you of the wisdom of God. Empty yourself and like a child depend wholly on Christ as a child on his father and you will experience that faith that moves mountain. Jesus scolded Thomas to stop doubting and believe. This is because Thomas requires a logical proof to believe that the Lord has risen. He extolled the centurion for his faith in believing that his servant will be healed even without having Jesus physically present or performing any physical sign. He said: Just speak the Word, and my servant will be totally healed. Do you believe the Word, or do you require a sign – a proof?

Faith comes from hearing, believing and acting on the Word. The Bible says that faith comes by hearing, and hearing by God's word. (Rom. 10:17). Your faith in Christ comes from the word of God implanted in you. It came like a mustard seed that is nurtured so that it grows to become the biggest of all. As long as you are a believer in Christ Jesus, you already have faith but it needs to grow. The Apostle once begged Jesus:

Lord, "Increase our faith!" He replied that if you have faith that is as little as a mustard seed, you can speak to this mulberry tree, 'Be uprooted and be thrown into the sea, and it will obey you (Luke. 17:5-6).

From the above text one will understand that to make you faith work or grow, you must listen to the word of God and act on it. That is to say that the faith that is already in you will grow and work only when you put it to action: work with it. In my early days in the ministry I had the problem of believing the Word of God I speak unto miracle. This is because many of those I am supposed to look upon, I came to know, never believed the Word is life and active and can cause miracle to happen. I mistakenly followed in that direction until on a particular occasion when the Holy Spirit wants to cause a change. This came as an answer to the prayer I made asking the Lord to reveal to me the power of the Word. One of my sisters in the Lord was struck down by an unknown illness that kept her bedridden for some days. She sent a message across that I should come to pray for her healing. I refused to go and sent a message back that they should take her to a hospital. This is because I never believed that my prayer would work. I don't want the sister to depend on my prayer for healing since I don't believe it either. But the sister insisted and continues sending one message after another because, as she told me later, the illness was not responding to treatment. When I couldn't refuse the invitation any longer. I went inside my room knelt down in humility and prayer 'Lord show your power like in the days of old' when I got to the sister's house, I held her hands, look up to heaven and prayed in power, rebuking the spirit of infirmity. In few minutes, the sister started vomiting and immediately after vomiting, she stood and began to walk. It was dramatic. It was marvelous. It was great. I couldn't help but praise the mighty name of God. This changed my whole idea of prayer. From then, my perception about prayer changed. I now believe that when I pray, He listens and he answers, Alleluia. This opened the way to so many other great works in my ministry. Don't allow negative teachings and words from faithless and confused teachers to weaken your faith. No matter the condition and situation believe God for a change. Read the Word of God, confess it, believe it and act on it, for miracle still happens.

DESIRE, ASK, BELIEVE AND YOU WILL RECEIVE

"Have faith in God," Jesus answered. I am telling you the truth if any of you speak to this mountain: Be uprooted, cast yourself into the sea, and does not have doubt in his mind but believes that what he speaks will happen, it will happen for him. So, I tell you the truth, whatsoever you requested for in prayer believe that you already have it, and it will become yours. (Mark 11;22 – 24).

I have taken time to prepare you for this time – a time to receive. You are ready to receive these divine blessings for it is all yours. You have been cleansed by the Word I have spoken to you. (John 15:3) You are a child of inheritance. All you need to do is to desire it, ask for it, believe that you have received it and it shall be yours. Stop crying, stop complaining, just receive, "for everyone who asks receives; he who seeks finds; and to him who knocks, the door will be opened". (See Matt. 7:7). Christ has done everything. You are not redoing it or bringing it to existence or creating it again or paying the prize for it – no, it is already there for you. Just ask and you will be given. If you don't ask you will not receive. Please don't desire crumbs like the Canaanite woman (See Matt. 15:27) or the pods that the pigs eat like the prodigal son (See Luk. 15:16) but desire great things like a Prince or Princess. When you desire great things like a Prince or Princess. When you desire it, ask for it and believe it is already yours and you shall get it. Have you heard the Word of God say that the desire of the righteous shall be granted? (See Prov. 10:24). The death of Jesus upon the for of Calvary qualified you for this inheritance. So, don't condemn yourself for Christ has not condemned you, just with open hands keep on asking so that you will keep on receiving. If you don't ask you will blame yourself. The Bible says "Until now you have not asked anything in my name; ask and you will receive, so that your joy may be complete." (John 16:24) and in John chapter 15 verse 16, Jesus says, "the Father will give you anything you ask him in my name". are you still waiting? It is time to receive; call upon the Lord and He will answer you, and show you great and mighty things, which you do not know. (See Jer. 33:3).

When you pray; ask or decree anything and believed that is already done, it is immediately established in the spiritual realm. Its manifestation in the physical can be instantaneous and dramatic or it can take little time to take full effect. But one thing sure is that it already done. Believe it and enjoy it. In Mark 11:12-14, Jesus cursed a fig tree saying, "may no one ever eat your fruit again!" This is because it was full of leaves but there were no figs on it. After causing this fig tree at that moment, it was still standing evergreen but Jesus being a man of faith knew that the tree is already dead. The disciples didn't understand what happened because they were looking at the physical and are still seeing the tree evergreen not knowing that it was already dead. Mark Chapter 11:20-22 reads.

In the morning the next day, as they passed across the fig tree he cursed, the apostles noticed it has withered completely from the roots. Then Peter recalled what Lord Jesus said to the fig tree on the previous day and shouted: Look, Lord! This fig tree you cursed has died! And Lord Jesus told to the disciples, "have faith in Almighty God."

Wow! It takes faith to cause a miracle to happen. Jesus saw and perceived the miracle the previous day when he decreed it, but the disciple only saw it when its physical manifestation came. As they jumped and began to rejoice for the physical signs they saw, Jesus exhorted to them have faith in God, for a man of faith would have seen the miracle the previous day it happened and not waiting for signs. The miracle happened the very time he declared it but they couldn't see. Which group do you belong? I love the way of Jesus and I do it the way of Jesus. I see it afar just like Balaam in Numbers Chapter 23 verse 15 to 17. Balaam cried "The oracle of Balaam son of Boer, the oracle of one whose eye sees clearly… I see him, but not now; I behold him, but not near. A star will rise out of Israel; a scepter will come out of Jacob ….

Jesus said if you ask, just believe and it will be yours. Abraham our father in the faith did the same many years ago when God called him and declared his barrenness over, Abraham perceived the miracle immediately. Even though that it took 17 years to come to pass. Abraham staggered not for he knows that the Miracle has already taken place. The Bible says:

Abraham did not stagger at the promise of the Almighty God through unbelief; but he was very strong in faith, giving all glory to God; And being fully persuaded that, what God had promised, he was also able to accomplish. (Romans 4:20).

Even though Abraham was getting very old and his body getting very weak, he didn't shake or waver because he knows that the miracle is already done, and that "time" cannot withhold or change it.

Even the thought that his body was as good as dead— he was about a hundred years old – and that Sarah's womb was dead too did not shake his faith. (Romans 4:19).

Today we sing of Abraham's Blessings. Everything about him is Blessing. This is because he through faith received ALL THINGS. Beloved, you too can be enriched with these heavenly riches and blessings but you have to develop a miracle-working faith, and the best way is to begin to live by the Word, act on the Word, and "do the Word" for it never fails (see Isaiah 10:55). The Bible says if it delays, wait for it will surely come.

And the Lord God said to me: Write down this vision and make it very plain on a tablet, that he may run who reads it because this vision is but for an appointed time: But at the very end it will come to pass, and it will not delay. Though if it tarries, wait for it: because it will surely come to pass, it will not tarry. (Hab. 2:2-4).

BE A PERSISTENT KNOCKER

The Blind Bartimaeus in Mark chapter 10:46-52 refused to give in to the distractions of the outside world even though they were too hard on him, he continued knocking until he got what he wanted and the door was opened to him. People may try to distract you; forces may try to prevent you; spirits may tell you it I not going to work; logic and philosophy may say it is not possible; History may say it has never happened before; doubts may come, worldly wisdom may suggest otherwise but don't give in to all these distractions for the Almighty God is very able to do much more abundantly above all that we may ask or think (imagine), according to the power that works in us, (Eph. 3:20) and God is not a man, that he should lie, nor a son of man, that he should change his mind. Does he speak and then not act? Does he promise and not fulfill? (Numbers 23:19) Listen to me, don't allow anybody or anything or even your won spirit to discourage you. Raise your head up above all distraction and keep on asking, keep on knocking until the door opens. Blind Bartimaeus knocked even harder when people and situation tried to distract. The Bible says:

when Blind Bartimaeus heard that it was Jesus Christ, he started crying out, saying: Lord Jesus, Son of David, please have mercy me! And many people warned him to keep quiet; but he raised his voice all the more: Lord Jesus Son of David, have mercy on me! Then, Lord

Jesus stood still and beckoned him to come. (Mark 10:47-49).

To the people around Blind Bartimaeus was a noisemaker, he was confused, he doesn't understand, he was a poor beggar who doesn't know anything but the Lord understands the yearning of this heart and healed his wounds forever. Learn to knock and keep on knocking until the poor opens. The Lord listens, He understands and He answers. "No one is disgraced who waits for Him, but only those who lightly break faith." (Ps. 25:3NAB). You ought to pray and continue to pray till every obstacle melts. Jesus says: men always ought to pray and not lose heart (Luke 18:1). The Lord wants you to continue to remind him of his promises until he fulfills it all and makes you the pride of the nation.

Upon your wall O Jerusalem, I have stationed watchmen, they will never keep quiet day or night. All those who call on the Lord God, rest not and don't give him rest until he establishes Jerusalem and makes her the pride of the world. (Is. 62:6).

Doctors, after series of tests recommended major operation for a child who mistakenly swallowed a piece of mental. Her mother happened to be a member of our prayer group. When she told me the story, I encouraged her to take the child for the operation but she refused and persistently asked for prayers. I was moved by her insistence on one occasion she was following me around. I stopped and asked her what she wanted. She made this statement: I totally respect the position of doctors, but I know that God can as well heal even without the doctors. I prayed for her and she left. The operation was never conducted again. The Lord healed the child. The doctors couldn't believe it. They conducted other tests and this was confirmed. It is the Lord's doing! The woman knows how to ask and was persistent in asking and the Lord granted her heart desire. Never lose heart no matter the situation, even when men have no solution, God can do it.

HAVE THE SAME MIND THAT IS IN CHRIST JESUS

A Sister told me one day that she will invoke Holy Ghost fire to consume the young girls of her village and she invited me to join in the prayers. Why? Because they sent a task force to carry away her property for not attending a communal work. When I rebuked her, she couldn't understand it? She had thought I should understand that they were wrong in their action. Actually, it was not all her fault because there was misinformation somewhere. But is that enough reason why the Holy Ghost Fire should consume her village youths? By the way, will the Holy Spirit ever do such kind of work? This is the kind of Prayer Fr. Stephen Njoku called witchcraft prayer in his book "You Be An intercessor." I totally agree with him in condemning this kind of prayer because the Holy Spirit is a Spirit of love. He comes to dispel darkness and establish the light of Christ in our hearts. It is not used for human destruction. All we do is to direct the fire of the Holy Ghost against demons and forces of darkness and not for human destruction.

The Roman soldiers crushed Jesus with pains and agony and at the height of it crucified him on the cross and all he could do or say is Father, forgive them because they are ignorant of what they are doing. He rebuked James and John when they wanted to call fire from heaven to destroy the Samaritan village for not allowing them to pass through their village.

Jesus sent disciples ahead of him, who went into a village in Samaria to get things prepared for him; but the people there resisted him because he was going to Jerusalem. When his disciples James and John heard this, they asked him, Master, do you want us to call down fire from heaven to destroy all of them? But Jesus Christ rebuked them, and they went through another village. (Luke. 9:52-56).

The heart of Jesus is a heart of love. It is filled with mercy and compassion. In order to receive and continue to enjoy these riches of the kingdom, you ought to have the same kind of mind that is in Christ Jesus. (See Phil. 2:5). Always say again and again, Jesus meek and humble of heart make my heart like unto thine. In Luke chapter 15, the elder brother of the prodigal son denied himself the good feast of the kingdom because of bitterness and rancour. You must flush yourself of these things in order to fully enjoy the true blessing. The Bible says:

Do not model your behaviour on the contemporary world, but let the renewing of your mind transform you, so that you may discern for yourselves what is the will of God – what is good and acceptable and mature. (Rom. 12:2).

...put aside your mortal flesh, which belongs to your old life, and has been defiled by your illusory desires. Let your mind be renewed in spirit so that you can put on the New Man which was created according to God in uprightness and true holiness. (Eph. 4: 22 – 24).

Sin and wickedness destroyed man's relationship with God, corrupt the mind, and cripple the power of reasoning. It makes one reason negatively such that all that comes out of him are not only evil but also failure and hopelessness. This is because once one begins to live a life of sin, he begins to avoid God, who is the author of all goodness and has no evil in him. This situation attacks and destroys one's faith, trust, and belief in God. Such that one no longer believes the power of Jesus to save, instead he sticks to his own strength, style and ideas. Unless such a mind is healed and renewed and such a person delivered from the power of sin, it will be difficult for him to appreciate the healing power of God. Yes – because he no longer believes in God but in his own logic and ideas. Even though he goes to Church and attend fellowship, he denies the power therein. This is the situation that was portrayed in the Parable of the talent. The wicked and lazy servant went and dug a hole in the ground and hid his master's money. This is because he never believed in him. To the servant, the master is a wicked man and has nothing to offer. So, he tried to avoid him. Immediately he received money from his master instead of thinking how to make good use of it, something in him told him that it was a trap from his master instead of thinking how to make good use of it, something in him told him that it was a trap from his master and he acted on that. The other two servants saw it from the positive side and it translated into more blessings for them. (See Matt. 25: 13 – 20). All things are possible to him that believes, don't allow sin or evil to destroy your faith in God. It is the worst thing that can happen to a man on earth.

How do you receive it when good things happen to your neighbour? Is it with joy and happiness or with envy and jealousy? What do you do when you are to contest for a position with someone else? Do you send Holy Ghost fire to destroy him so that the position will be yours or pray him into the wall of God? Love is the basis to receive. Without love, it will be very difficult to receive from God, because God is Love. A generous heart receives beyond measure from God. Open your hands and it will be filled and the Bible says: a full measure, pressed down, shaken together, and overflowing, will be poured into your lap (Luke 6:38). Be a source of blessing to others and your jar of oil will never run dry. (cf.1 King 17:12-16).

THE POWER OF PRAISES

Praise God at all times especially when the going gets tough and nothing seems to work. Praise has the power to provoke God's mercy and healing. In fact a man who knows how to praise will always receive because Praises is an expression of faith that what we asked for has already been received even though we cannot see it Job in the midst of his problems and difficulties raised his head up and began to praise God saying: I know that my Redeemer lives,

I know that my Redeemer is alive and that in the very end, he will stand on the earth. And after this my skin is destroyed, yet in this my flesh, I will see the almighty God; I will see him myself with my very own eye -- I, and not any other person. My heart yearns inside me! (Job 19:25 – 27).

When Paul and Silas were thrown into prison, the Bible says they prayed and sang until the whole prison began to shake. Their praises caused a severe earthquake that shook the foundations of the prison, doors were thrown open, iron bars cracked and set loose and every chain and ties were broken and the children of God were set free – the power of Praise. (See Acts 16:25 – 34). Whenever you prayed and it seems that the answers to such prayers are not forthcoming, raise your head up and begin to worship God in Praises. Go on and on, praising God, thanking him for answers received, even though you have not seen it. Believe it, affirm it, praise God for it and it will be yours.

There are so many cases of divine healing and miracle, taking place in mightily during praise. The Glory of God descended in power during praise ministration in our ministry one day and overlook the whole assembly to such an extent that a paralyzed woman got her healing instantly and began to dance around even without knowing it. The woman who came to realize that she is no longer paralyzed but healed only after the praises. She confessed that she has gone to places seeking for healing all to no avail. Learn to praise God because obstacles and mountain melt when we do. The Bible says;

Through Lord Jesus Christ, therefore, let us continue to offer the almighty God a sacrifice of praise – which is the fruit of our lips that confess his name. (Heb. 13:15).

Finally, always pray for the will of God for your life. The will of God is the best for you. Don't insist on your own way. Relax in His palms because He is able to take you to Glory. Surrender to Jesus and follow Him day by day and you will never suffer lack. To those who follow Jesus, He says, they will "receive a hundred times as much in this present age.... and the age to come, eternal life." (Mark 10:30). This is my prayer for you, "that you may prosper in all things and be in health, just as your soul prospers." (3 John 1:2). May this be your portion, as you make effort to dwell in His presence day by day.